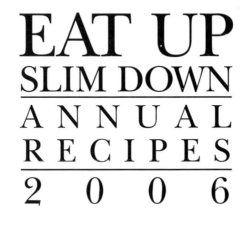

EAT UP
SLIM DOWN
ANNUAL
RECIPES
2 0 0 6

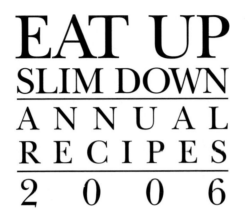

EAT UP
SLIM DOWN
ANNUAL
RECIPES
2006

150 Simply Delicious Recipes
for Permanent Weight Loss

RODALE

Portions of this book have been adapted from material that has appeared in *Prevention* magazine and in the Rodale book entitled *The Sugar Solution*.

Printed in the United States of America
Rodale Inc. makes every effort to use acid-free ⊗, recycled paper ♻.

"Choosing to Become a Weight-Loss Winner" on pages 1 through 10 is adapted from *The Perfect Fit Diet* by Lisa Sanders, Rodale Inc. © 2004 by Lisa Sanders.

Book design by Kristen Morgan Downey
Interior and cover photography credits are on page 257.

Front cover recipe: Jenn's Easy No-Bake Prune Pie (page 229)

ISBN-13 978-1-59486-240-3 hardcover
ISBN-10 1-59486-240-0 hardcover

2 4 6 8 10 9 7 5 3   hardcover

RODALE
LIVE YOUR WHOLE LIFE™

We inspire and enable people to improve their lives and the world around them

For more of our products visit **rodalestore.com** or call 800-848-4735

Contents

Special Thanks

In grateful appreciation to all the supporters and sponsors of the Eat Up Slim Down Recipe Sweepstakes, we would like to thank . . .

The companies that so generously provided the terrific prizes for the sweepstakes:
Capresso, CDN, Chantal, Kuhn Rikon, Meadowsweet Kitchens, Messermeister, Smellkiller, William Bounds

The product representatives who were so generous with their time and talents:
Elena Shanoff Kokosa from Field & Associates

And sincere, heartfelt thanks . . .
. . . to all of the readers of www.eatupslimdown.com and www.prevention.com who were kind enough to share their delicious recipes, clever tips, and inspiring stories of weight-loss success for this book. We salute you and wish you continued success.

. . . to the eight weight-loss winners who shared their stories of success with us in personal profiles: Christina Alderman, Paula Gebhart, Tessie Konya, Linda Lindsey, Barbara Orland, Margaret Roach, Trudy Rogers-Moore, and Danny Schwartz.

Acknowledgments

A very special thank you to everyone who had a hand in creating *Eat Up Slim Down Annual Recipes 2006*.

Pamela Adler
Carol Angstadt
Miriam Backes
JoAnn Brader
Tara Chu
Melissa Dapkewicz
Melissa DeMayo
Christine Detris
Kristen Morgan Downey
Kathleen Hanuschak, RD
Marilyn Hauptly
Joely Johnson
Fran Kriebel
Lisa Leventer
Mitch Mandel
Lonnie McDonald
Joan Parkin
Stacy Petrovich
Miriam Rubin
Kathy Schuessler
Eva Seibert
Kimberly Tweed
Diane Vezza
Shannon Yeakel
Shea Zukowski

Contributors

This book is a compilation of the delicious and creative recipes sent to us by weight-loss winners across the United States, and even beyond. The number of recipes we received was so great, it was a difficult task choosing 150. But after a careful selection process, we managed to whittle it down. Here are this year's recipe contributors. We salute their innovative efforts in the kitchen, and hope you'll enjoy eating up and slimming down with their recipes!

Introduction

If you've recently gained a few unwanted pounds (or more than a few), welcome to the fifth edition of *Eat Up Slim Down*. Gathered in these pages is a wealth of useful new information, practical tips, and sound advice designed to help you to shed those extra pounds, and keep them off for good. Think of this book as your dieting companion.

As you've come to expect from this series, you will find page after page of the latest and greatest in health and fitness advice, guaranteed to inspire you to continue on your weight-loss journey or maybe even begin the one you've been trying to start for so long.

In the first chapter, we show you how to choose a personal food plan tailored to your personality and weight-loss style with guidance from a new book, *The Perfect Fit Diet*. In chapter two, we tackle a growing health problem, high-normal blood sugar or prediabetes, and show how it is tied into those pesky pounds around your waist. In chapter three, we help you get a handle on the one factor that can undermine anyone who wants to lose weight—that dreadful "H" word, *hunger*—and we share specific tips to help you better understand the reasons you may be overeating in the first place. And then we put it all together in chapter four with delicious, healthful, calorie-smart approaches to each meal.

As if that's not enough, you will also find plenty of inspiration by reading advice from people just like you. These real-life weight-loss winners have let nothing stop them from reaching their goals. A car accident caused chronic back pain for a once very active Trudy Rogers-Moore from Sarina, Ontario, and made it impossible for her to avoid packing on the pounds. But after finding the right equipment, Trudy was able to drop those extra pounds and has kept them off for 2 years and counting! Just wait until you see the before and after pictures for all of the weight-loss winners—they are amazing!

And, of course, we haven't forgotten the recipes. We have 150 new and fabulous calorie-wise recipes contributed by readers just like you. Delicious *and* easy to prepare, there are outstanding dishes to make for every meal and every occasion. We know you'll love adding meals like Madras Orange Chicken with Ginger Fried Rice, Pork Loin with Apple Cider Glaze, and Spinach Stuffed Shells to your dinner menu. Plus, you'll be able to savor dessert again with Angelic

Strawberry Trifle, Banana Sunflower Cookies, and Peachy Frozen Yogurt to help you stick to your diet plan. We've tested each one in our test kitchen, so you are sure to find an appetizer, entree, or dessert that helps combat those pesky cravings without sending you into calorie overload. Each recipe is complete with calorie, fat, carbohydrate, and diet exchange info, too, so that you will be able to fit it into whichever diet you and your doctor have decided is best for you to follow.

Congratulations on taking the first step toward becoming an all new you! We can't wait to hear your success stories and to try your recipes for weight loss. Please visit www.eatupslimdown.com to share them with us.

Choosing to Become a Weight-Loss Winner

Taking the First Step

For many people, losing weight—and keeping it off—is a constant struggle. That's because the underlying message of many diets is that you must repress your desire for and deprive yourself of the foods you love because if you don't, you just might devour any and all food left in sight. It's easy to fear becoming a hopeless, bottomless pit.

Of course, this kind of thinking certainly isn't productive—and it also isn't true. No one's hunger is bottomless, and the fact that you're reading this book shows that you are neither hopeless nor out of control.

A diet that promotes negative self-talk is unlikely to work for long. Rather, long-lasting changes in eating habits can only come through being kind to yourself, being

mindful about what you are doing and why, and being willing to act on your own behalf. Figuring out what you really need is the real key to weight-loss success, and this book was written to help you do just that.

In this chapter, adapted in part from the work of Dr. Lisa Sanders and her recent book *The Perfect Fit Diet,* you'll find the information you need to choose the right diet to fit your unique preferences and lifestyle.

We'll also discuss some problems dieters commonly face within each type of diet. By trouble-shooting these roadblocks ahead of time, you'll be better prepared to meet these challenges as they arise so that you can reach your weight-loss goals more easily.

After you've chosen your diet plan, you'll

1

find this book offers a delicious range of recipes from other weight-loss winners just like you. Plus, you'll find the calorie, fat, carb, and diet exchange information is listed at the bottom of each recipe. Using this information, you'll have great dishes to keep you slim and satisfied no matter which diet you choose to follow.

Every Diet Works for Someone

Anyone who tries to lose weight—and that's 83 million Americans every year—confronts aisle after aisle of diet books offering competing and often contradictory strategies: Eat in the Zone. Eat low-fat or no-fat. Eat high-carb. Eat low-carb. Eat right for your blood type, for your body type, for your personality. Bust sugar. Think thin.

Do any of these diets actually work? Dr. Sanders has been investigating what science actually knows about obesity and nutrition. Along with a team of investigators from Yale and Stanford, she spent the past 3 years analyzing more than 700 studies on diet and weight loss, dating back to 1917. In the process, Sanders was struck by a surprising pattern that seemed to defy conventional wisdom: Every one of these diets worked—for some people. So, perhaps the key to successful weight loss lies not in the specific diet, nor even in the person who's trying to lose weight, but in matching the dieter to the right diet. This means that you can find a diet that will work for you.

Consider Your Lifestyle

What you eat, how you eat, and when you eat are all part of your lifestyle. And despite what

WHY YOUR FRIEND LOSES WEIGHT AND YOU DON'T

How many times has this happened to you? You meet a friend you haven't seen in a while, and she looks great. After years of trying one diet or the other, she has finally found the right one, she says. She gets to eat the food she loves, she's never hungry, and she's losing weight like crazy. Before you know it, you're on the same diet, but it doesn't seem so great. You don't like the food. You're not losing weight, just patience. You wonder, "What's wrong with me?"

There's nothing wrong with you, and there's nothing necessarily wrong with the diet. You're just learning a basic truth about dieting: One size does not fit all.

nutrition buffs would like to believe, these are probably not the most important issues in your life, but rather they must compete with other compelling aspects of your day: your job, your family, and all the other pleasures and obligations that make up a life. But the life into which you integrate your diet has a profound effect on how well that diet works. Therefore, you need to take your real life into consideration when you choose and design your diet.

Usually, when a diet gets out of hand and

causes weight gain, it is due not only to the foods eaten but also to when, where, why, and how the food is eaten. As adults—over-committed, wildly busy, terrifically stressed—we have developed eating habits that interfere with the natural mechanisms that regulate when and how much we eat.

Too Busy to Eat Right?

Stressed-out and busy workers or parents can find themselves too busy to eat. Maybe they grab a quick snack, or maybe they just tough it out, but in either case chances are good that they're starving by the time their next meal rolls around. When it does, they sit down and in an instant consume their entire meal and more—often much more. The mechanisms that might otherwise tell them that they have had enough are silenced by their outsize hunger, and they overeat. Sound familiar?

And then there is the opposite problem: Some people eat when they aren't hungry. Maybe they are stressed, bored, or tired—but they are not hungry. The body treats these snacks differently from the snacks you eat when you are hungry. Snacks you eat when you are hungry usually cause you to eat less at your next meal than you otherwise would. Snacks that you eat when you are not hungry don't do that. Your body just doesn't count them when it's doing the math about how many calories you've eaten. So food you eat when you're not hungry ends up being just extra calories.

Looking for the Right Diet

All diets work by eliminating or reducing one or more types of food. Below are sketches of the three basic types of diets and a rundown of some of the most popular versions of these.

Low-Fat Diets

Overall, these diets reduce fat intake to 10 to 35 percent of calories consumed. They limit foods such as meat and dairy while emphasizing naturally low-fat fruits, vegetables, and grains.

A well-known example is Dr. Dean Ornish's diet, which reduces fat intake to 10 percent of your daily calories (15 to 25 grams) and entirely eliminates meat, fats and oils, chicken, and fish. Legumes, grains, fat-free dairy, fruits, and vegetables are allowed. Dr. Ornish asserts that if you change the type of food you eat, you don't need to be as concerned about portion size.

Weight Watchers is another respected, low-fat eating plan; it allows a more moderate fat intake than Dr. Ornish's plan does. Based on a system of food choices, it offers wholesome selections from all the food groups, along with the occasional treat, adding up to a low-fat plan. Weight Watchers provides tools and support to the dieter in many ways, but it is most famous for its group meetings.

Another moderate low-fat plan comes from the American Heart Association (AHA). The AHA offers a set of guidelines for healthy eating and weight loss, rather than a specific diet, so it's easy to adapt for practically anyone. The plan promotes eating habits for good heath overall, with particular emphasis on reducing your risk factors for heart attack and stroke. AHA guidelines encourage you to eat plenty of grains, fruits, and vegetables, along with moderate amounts of low-fat and fat-free dairy, healthful fats, fish, legumes, skinless poultry, and lean meats. Under the guidelines, you are to avoid foods high in calories or low in nutrition, and you balance the occasional high-fat splurge or salty snack with lower-fat foods such as steamed vegetables or fruit.

Low-Calorie or Calorie-Counting Diets

These diets, which focus on variety and promote foods that keep you full longer, can help you eat less while keeping hunger under control.

One such diet is The Volumetrics Weight-Control Plan, developed by Barbara Rolls, PhD. In Volumetrics, the focus is on foods and prepared dishes with higher water and fiber contents, including fruits, vegetables, and whole grains, along with soups and stews (which are rich in broth and juices). Eating satisfying portions of these high-volume foods will help you feel full and content, even while you reduce your daily calorie intake.

Low-Carb Diets

Another popular category, these diets recommend eating more protein and fat and fewer carbohydrates—but when it's all added up, you're still reducing calorie intake while eating satisfying foods.

On some low-carb diets, you can eat as much high-saturated-fat foods (such as cheeseburgers, minus the buns, and bacon) as you want, but you can't eat most fruits, vegetables, breads, and cereals. Other low-carb diets focus on eating healthy fats and limiting refined carbohydrates, including white bread, cakes, and cookies.

As the name says, low-carb diets limit consumption of carbs and provide plenty of protein. The Atkins Diet and the South Beach Diet are the most popular examples of low-carb plans.

Matching the Dieter to the Diet

Here are some general guidelines for who does best on which type of diet. The key is to find a diet you can live with for the long term. The diet needs to suit who you are and how and what you enjoy eating. If your diet doesn't include foods that you like, you are less likely to stay on the wagon.

You'll do best on a low-fat diet if you . . .

- don't eat a lot of meat.
- enjoy fruits, vegetables, and whole grain foods.
- need volume to feel full.
- eat meals regularly (about every 4 to 5 hours).
- don't travel or eat out frequently. (Fresh fruits and veggies and whole grains can be hard to find, and restaurants tend to use lots of fat.)
- are willing to have your cholesterol levels checked. (If your triglycerides go up, which they do for some people, this is probably not the right diet for you.)

You'll do best on a low-calorie or calorie-counting diet if you . . .

- need a lot of variety.
- don't mind measuring portion sizes.
- find yourself standing in front of the refrigerator trying to identify the food you are craving.
- can eat only a little of something you like.
- have given up on diets because you were bored with the foods they offered.

You'll do best on a low-carbohydrate diet if you . . .

- enjoy eating meat, cheese, and eggs.
- find it hard to feel full without eating these foods.

- don't care much about variety.
- are able to limit fruits and vegetables.
- can say goodbye to breads, pastas, and sweets.
- travel or eat out a lot. (You can always find meat or fish and a salad, the prototypical meal of this diet.)
- are willing to have your cholesterol levels checked. (If they go up, which they do for some people, this is probably not the right diet for you.)

Avoiding Diet Pitfalls

Each type of diet has its own danger zone—a time when a dieter is most likely to slip up, and maybe even give up. Have you ever been there? We're betting you have. After all, experts say that most dieters will fall off the wagon within the first couple of weeks.

Below we identify the most common trouble spots associated with the three types

CRASH DIETS DON'T WORK

People who lose 5 to 10 pounds in a week lose water, not fat, so try to lose only a pound or two a week. Depending on how much you have to lose, it could take as long as 6 months to lose 10 percent of your body weight in a healthy way, but that means you're more likely to maintain your new weight.

of diets: low-fat, low-calorie, and low-carb. To help you navigate the danger zones, we asked weight-loss experts and in-the-trenches dieters for their escape strategies. Here's their best advice to help you beat the odds.

Low-Fat Diets

Try to avoid constant hunger. It's a fact: The less fat you eat, the less satisfied you'll be. Why? A study at the University of California, Davis, found that dietary fat stimulates the release of cholecystokinin, a hormone that is believed to enhance satiety—that sense of having eaten enough. And let's face it: Fat makes food taste good.

On a low-fat diet, then, it's fiber to the rescue. The secret is to begin by getting some good-tasting, healthy fat, such as olive oil, in your diet, says Dr. Rolls. Then incorporate

lots of high-fiber foods such as legumes, brown rice, and fruits. Eating a low-fat, high-fiber diet that satisfies your hunger leads to three times greater weight loss than a low-fat diet alone, according to a recent review of published studies.

Don't fall for "low-fat" labels. "Reducing your fat intake may stimulate your cravings for sweets," says Stephen P. Gullo, PhD, author of *Thin Tastes Better.* And many dieters satisfy this craving by reaching for reduced-fat cakes, cookies, and chocolate. "The problem," says Wahida Karmally, DrPh, RD, director of nutrition at Columbia University Medical Center, "is that a reduced-fat Oreo and a regular Oreo have about the same calories."

What should you do instead? Go natural. "Choose foods that are naturally low in fat, not those that have been engineered to be low-fat," says Karmally. She recommends yummy and satisfying natural sweets such as strawberry and banana smoothies and fruits such as watermelon and mangoes as an alternative to reduced-fat confections that are neither a caloric nor a nutritional bargain.

Calorie-Counting or Low-Calorie Diets

Avoid the extreme. Limiting your calorie intake is the surest, most basic weight-loss method around—unless you go too far. "Most people are looking for instant results, so they cut out way too many calories," says Molly Kimball, RD, sports and lifestyle nutritionist at Ochsner's Elmwood Fitness Center in New Orleans. "I had one client who ran and lifted weights for 2 hours a day on nothing but a Luna Bar for breakfast and some high-fiber cereal for lunch." Blinded by hunger in the late afternoon, she would fill

WISE WORDS TO DIET BY, FROM LISA SANDERS, MD

Based on my research and clinical experience, I have developed a number of principles that apply to everyone trying to lose weight, no matter which diet they're following. Here are just a few.

Weight gain is not a moral failure. For generations, dieters have been told that weight control is all about self-control and willpower. In fact, losing weight has nothing to do with willpower and everything to do with finding a diet that fits. Guilt is weight-loss enemy number one. You don't have to be a paragon of willpower, but you do have to learn not to give in to despair and self-destructive bingeing when you lapse.

Life is unfair. You've long suspected it; now science has proved it to be true. We inherit factors that determine how easy or hard it will be for each of us to gain or lose weight. Genes aren't destiny, but you can't pretend they don't exist. Work with what you've got. It's the only body you'll ever have.

Eat when you're hungry, not when you're starving. Many dieters believe that it's good to feel hungry because that means they're eating less. Yes and no. When you allow yourself to get too hungry, your body thinks it's starving. Then, when you finally allow yourself to eat, the cues that tell you that you have had enough are drowned out by your body's "panic" at the prospect of starvation. To stay in control, aim to eat three meals a day, plus snacks.

Get some satisfaction. Eating is one of our most primal life drives, and like sex, eating is engineered around satisfaction. Diets that deny you that satisfaction don't work, for the simple reason that you can't stay on them. Make sure that you eat foods that you enjoy, and make sure that you enjoy the foods you eat.

Deal with stress—don't add to it. Stress makes most of us overeat high-fat foods, and stress hormones change our body's metabolism and cause us to gain weight. Since we all have stress in our lives, much of weight management really comes down to stress management.

Exercise smart. What few dieters understand is that, like food, exercise has to fit your preferences. Otherwise you won't stick with it.

up on ice cream and trail mix and ultimately went up two dress sizes within a year.

Instead, try to play by the rules. The unfortunate reality is that crash diets don't lead to long-term solutions. "Your body just isn't going to play along if you try to get by on only 600 calories a day," says Kimball. In fact, it's going to revolt and make weight loss more difficult by burning fewer calories. The old rule about losing no more than 1 to

REV YOUR METABOLISM: DRINK WATER

From cabbage soup to South Beach, popular diets agree on one thing: Water helps weight loss. To put this long-standing claim to the test, researchers in Germany measured the resting metabolisms of 14 men and women before and after they drank just over 16 ounces of water. Within 10 minutes, each person's metabolism began to rise. After 40 minutes, the volunteers' average calorie-burning rate was 30 percent higher, and it stayed elevated for more than an hour.

Researchers don't understand why, but they calculate that drinking eight 8-ounce glasses of water a day—the generally recommended amount—can burn off almost 35,000 calories a year, or about 10 pounds.

How much water you should add to your diet depends on your current consumption, says researcher Jens Jordan, MD. Consuming a total of 8 to 12 cups daily is safe, he says, and cool water works best because part of the increased calorie burn occurs as the body warms the liquid to body temperature.

2 pounds a week still holds; that generally means eating about 500 fewer calories a day, but not cutting calories any lower than 1,200 a day.

Don't skip meals. "Not eating at regular intervals leaves you just as vulnerable to hunger pains as eating too few calories does," says Kimball. "And feeling hungry is the surest way to lose your motivation." Most people who skip meals end up eating more calories, not fewer.

In an attempt to slim down her 280-pound figure, Yolanda Ellison, 27, a computer programmer in Toledo, Ohio, would go all day without eating. "But by the time dinner rolled around, I'd devour every morsel of fried food I could get my hands on," says Ellison. As it turned out, she was eating more calories in that one meal than she would have eaten in three meals a day. Not surprisingly, she didn't shed an ounce.

Instead of starving and bingeing, concentrate on eating super-filling minimeals. "The first thing I tell my clients is that eating less doesn't mean not eating," says Kimball, who encourages women who are cutting calories to eat five or six small meals a day. Research has shown that snackers tend to have a lower risk of obesity than nonsnackers.

When planning your minimeals, you should choose foods that make you feel full while providing the least number of calories, says Dr. Rolls. "People tend to eat the same weight of food every day," she says. So fill up on foods that weigh a lot but have fewer calories, such as gazpacho, baked potatoes (without the high-fat toppings), fruits, and vegetables.

Get moving. When the needle on the scale won't budge, the most common response is to cut more calories. That may not be a smart move, because the less you weigh, the fewer calories your body requires.

For instance, a 300-pound woman most likely needs to consume about 3,000 calories a day to maintain her weight. So even if she eats 2,500 calories a day, she'll lose weight. After she loses more than 50 pounds, though, she'll have to further lower her calorie intake. But you can only go so low before your body hits starvation mode and refuses to shed more pounds.

Exercise will bust through the weight-loss plateau and help you keep the pounds off long-term. "In the beginning, I was so large that all I had to do was reduce my food intake slightly and the weight poured off me," says Janine DeVito, 33, who works for *Saturday Night Live* in New York City and used to weigh 300 pounds. But when the weight loss came to a screeching halt, "I felt like I couldn't limit my calories any more than I already was," says DeVito. That's when she dusted off an old treadmill in the basement, began walking every day, and finally got to her goal weight of 150 pounds.

Low-Carb Diets

Start off on the right foot by refueling often. Although it has captured the hearts, minds, and stomachs of at least 10 million Americans, this diet has an ugly side—carb withdrawal. Chief among the complaints of low-carb dieters are headaches, nausea, dizziness, and superlow energy. "By the end of the first day, I was shaking so badly I couldn't even hold a glass," says Sheila Smith, 36, a mother of three in Honolulu who has tried Atkins and other low-carb diets. "By the end of the second day, I was perspiring with a migraine, and by the third day, I quit."

When you're slogging through those early days, experts say it's imperative that you eat every 2 to 3 hours, even if you're not hungry. "This will prevent your blood sugar from dropping and reduce these side effects of a low-carb plan," says Kimball. If you're on a low-carb diet and your symptoms persist beyond 7 or 8 days, go ahead and move on to the second phase of the diet, which generally allows some fruits and whole grains, she advises.

Don't be trapped by the breakfast blues. Food burnout is a big problem for low-carbers, especially at breakfast. "I thought I'd vomit if I saw another egg," says

Steve Raupe, 40, of Oklahoma City. Dieters like Raupe find breakfast tough because there seem to be so few attractive low-carb options. "When people are confronted with the same type of food day after day, they get bored and often give up," says Kimball.

Spice up omelets with asparagus and goat cheese, scramble tofu with some veggies, or spread almond butter on a low-carb tortilla. Expand your notion of breakfast to include options from other meals, such as chicken salad, quiche, grilled steak or pork chops, and yogurt cucumber dip. Or borrow from other cultures where eggs and bacon aren't even considered.

Choose juicy, lower-calorie foods.
Even if you lose a dramatic amount of weight in the early stages of the diet, a recent study of 132 obese adults done at the Philadelphia Veterans Affairs Medical Center showed that after about six months of low-carbing it, weight loss tended to plateau. The culprits, most nutritionists say, are high-calorie foods such as bacon, salami, cheese, nuts, and peanut butter. "Many of my clients think that cutting carbs gives them a blank check to eat everything else," says Dr. Gullo.

Even though some of the diets themselves suggest that you don't have to worry about portion size, the reality is that calories count. Avoid foods that have low water content, such as butter, bacon, crackers, and nutrition bars, which tend to be very high in calories, suggests Jay Kenny, PhD, RD, director of nutritional research at Florida Pritikin Longevity Center and Spa in Aventura. Instead, choose lower-calorie, higher-water-content foods: shrimp (25 calories per ounce to bacon's 200), a skinless chicken breast (45 calories per ounce), or vegetables (fewer than 6 calories per ounce).

Balancing Your Blood Sugar

Learn to Keep Your Levels in Check

The average American consumes more than a pound of refined sugar a week. It sounds unbelievable, until you realize that sugar goes by more than 50 different names and is an ingredient in virtually all processed foods, from your morning doughnut to the ketchup on your burger.

Eat it (along with excess fat and calories), sit around, and you'll gain weight. This is the average American way of life, and it deserves a new warning label: Practicing this lifestyle could send another sugar—your blood sugar—into the danger zone.

The good news, however, is that losing even a few pounds provides numerous health benefits, including keeping your blood sugar stable.

Take our quiz (see "Is Your Blood Sugar in Balance?" on page 12) to see if your eating habits or lifestyle may be contributing to higher blood sugar levels, and read on to learn more about how to keep your blood sugar in balance for the long haul.

Why Blood Sugar Matters

Your body's primary source of fuel, blood sugar, plays a vital role in your physical and mental well-being. But when it rises even slightly above normal—thanks to excess body fat, lack of exercise, or genetics—your health, energy levels, and weight-loss efforts are jeopardized.

High-normal blood sugar is anything but
(continued on page 16)

IS YOUR BLOOD SUGAR IN BALANCE?

Only your doctor can help you answer this question for sure, but the following quiz can help you find out if your lifestyle protects you from high blood sugar or increases your risk. When you're done, read the brief explanation of each correct answer.

1. What do you usually eat for breakfast?
   a. high-fiber, whole grain cereal or oatmeal with fresh fruit and fat-free milk
   b. scrambled eggs and buttered toast
   c. pastry and a cup of coffee
2. How often do you watch TV?
   a. 1 hour a day
   b. 2 hours a day
   c. 2+ hours a day
3. What type of milk do you use most often?
   a. fat-free
   b. 2 percent
   c. whole milk
4. You need to get to the third floor of a high-rise. How do you get there?
   a. take the stairs and consider it a mini-workout
   b. take the stairs, but huff and puff a bit
   c. take the elevator
5. How much time do you spend each week on a physical activity that makes you sweat, such as walking or strenuous physical work?
   a. at least 150 minutes a week
   b. maybe 100 minutes a week
   c. usually zero minutes a week
6. When you make toast or a sandwich, what do you use?
   a. whole grain or multi-grain bread
   b. rye bread
   c. white bread
7. What do you sauté your veggies in?
   a. olive oil
   b. vegetable oil
   c. butter
8. How often do you lift weights or do some other type of resistance training (resistance bands, weight machines)?
   a. at least twice a week
   b. less than twice a week
   c. never
9. Which word best describes your ability to handle stress?
   a. excellent
   b. fair
   c. poor
10. How often do you eat beans?
    a. frequently—at least five times a week
    b. not very often—once or twice a week
    c. rarely, if ever
11. Do you smoke cigarettes?
    a. no
    b. a few a day
    c. 10 or more a day

12. How often do you eat each day (including snacks), and how large are those meals?
    a. five or six small meals a day
    b. three regular meals a day
    c. one or two large meals a day (especially dinner)

13. What's your alcoholic beverage of choice?
    a. don't drink
    b. wine
    c. a mixed drink or beer

14. How many hours of sleep do you usually get at night?
    a. 7½ hours or more
    b. between 6 and 7½ hours
    c. fewer than 6 hours

15. How often do you eat fish?
    a. five or more times a week
    b. once a week
    c. less than once a month

16. If you've had a fasting blood sugar test in the past year, the test result was:
    a. 99 milligrams/deciliter or lower
    b. 100 to 125 milligrams/deciliter
    c. 126 milligrams/deciliter or higher

17. Grab a tape measure and measure your waist. The result is:
    a. Less than 35 inches if you're a woman and less than 40 inches if you're a man
    b. 35 inches or more if you're a woman
    c. 40 inches or more if you're a man

SCORING

Give yourself 3 points for every "a" answer, 2 for every "b," and 1 for each "c."

41 points or more: Way to go! You're doing a great job to help your body process its blood sugar properly.

40 to 36 points: Nice work! You'll need to make just a few changes, especially if you're overweight or have other risk factors for high blood sugar. (See "Diabetes: Are You at Risk?" on page 17.)

35 to 31 points: Careful! This score is a bit on the so-so side, particularly if you have any of the risk factors for high blood sugar. (See "Diabetes: Are You at Risk?" on page 17.)

30 points or lower: Uh-oh! Call your doctor, who can test your blood sugar and recommend lifestyle changes.

HOW DID YOU DO?

The correct answer to every question is "a." Here's why.

1. Research shows that foods high in fiber, especially the soluble fiber in oatmeal, slow the absorption of glucose into the bloodstream, which helps control blood sugar levels.

2. Moderate exercise keeps muscle cells sensitive to insulin, the hormone that helps usher blood sugar into cells. Being an inactive couch potato makes your cells resist insulin, so blood sugar has trouble getting inside them and builds up in the bloodstream instead.

3. Even if you're overweight, consuming more low-fat dairy products, such as fat-free milk, could help reduce your risk of insulin resistance. In a 10-year study of 3,000 people, those who were overweight but got lots of dairy foods were 70 percent less likely to develop insulin resistance than those who avoided dairy. Milk sugar (lactose) is converted to blood sugar relatively slowly, which is good for blood sugar control and reducing insulin levels.

4. Climbing stairs burns extra calories and gives the heart a workout. It's one small way to help head off blood-sugar problems due to inactivity and overweight.

5. Exercising at a moderate intensity (walking briskly, for example) for just 30 minutes a day, five days a week, can reduce your risk of developing type 2 diabetes by 58 to 80 percent. Exercise is most protective if you also adopt a healthy diet. People who don't exercise at all increase their risk by 25 percent.

6. Whole grain bread is higher in fiber, which helps slow the rate at which sugar enters the bloodstream. Fiber also helps you maintain a healthy weight. To make sure you're getting whole wheat, look for the words "100 percent stoneground whole wheat," which should appear first on the ingredients list.

7. Olive oil and other good sources of monounsaturated fat (like flaxseed oil, avocados, and nuts) help people with blood-sugar problems indirectly, by reducing their risk of heart disease. In contrast, the saturated fat in butter and the trans fats in many margarines made with hydrogenated vegetable oils increase the risk of heart disease.

8. Resistance training builds muscle density. Stronger muscles that use more glucose. Along with aerobic exercise, increased muscle density also aids weight loss.

9. Chronic stress increases the risk of high blood sugar in two ways: by encouraging the body to store fat in the abdomen, where it impairs the liver's ability to control blood sugar, and by reducing muscle cells' sensitivity to insulin.

10. Beans are packed with soluble fiber, which blunts the entry of glucose into the

bloodstream. Soluble fiber also helps lower bad-guy LDLs.

11. Smoking is terrible for everyone's health, but it's especially destructive for people with high blood sugar. Compared to nonsmoking folks with type 2 diabetes, smokers with this disorder are three times more likely to die of cardiovascular disease.

12. Eating small meals frequently is better for blood sugar control than sitting down to occasional feasts. Large meals cause more glucose to enter the bloodstream quickly, taxing the ability of the pancreas to produce sufficient insulin.

13. In one study of nearly 80,000 people, women who drank beer or hard liquor one to four times a week were more likely to carry extra weight in the abdomen than women who didn't drink at all. However, wine was not associated with waist size in the study—which is significant because large waistlines increase diabetes risk—and may, in moderation, offer heart-protective effects that other alcoholic beverages do not.

14. Recent research found that people who averaged fewer than 6½ hours of sleep a night were found to have 40 percent greater insulin insensitivity—a major risk for developing diabetes—than people who slept 7½ hours or more.

15. In a Harvard School of Public Health study of over 5,000 women with type 2 diabetes, women who ate fish five or more times a week reduced their risk of developing heart disease by 64 percent compared with women who rarely ate fish. Women who ate fish once a week cut their risk by 40 percent.

16. Haven't been tested? A blood sugar test is an absolute must if you're 45 or older and overweight, or if you have any other risk factors for diabetes.

17. Research suggests that belly fat may be an even more potent risk factor for diabetes than weight alone. While experts aren't yet sure why, one theory is that insulin-resistant people store excess dietary fat in inappropriate places, such as in muscle cells and the liver, which makes it harder for their bodies to use sugar as fuel.

normal. Too high to be healthy yet too low to be called diabetes (it's often labeled prediabetes), high-normal blood sugar has long been overlooked by doctors and their patients alike. Yet an estimated 16 million Americans have it—including tens of thousands of children and teens. The rise of the high-normal blood sugar epidemic is the direct result of the rise in overweight and obesity in the United States.

More and more research links even "slightly" high blood sugar to food cravings, mood swings, and overweight, as well as pregnancy and fertility problems, heart attacks, stroke, full-blown type 2 diabetes, and even, early evidence suggests, some forms of cancer.

How Blood Sugar Problems Can Hamper Weight Loss

If you've tried to lose weight with no success, your blood sugar may be working against you.

High levels of insulin, the hormone that moves blood sugar out of the bloodstream and into cells and tissues, prevent fat breakdown, making weight loss difficult. At the other end of the spectrum, low blood sugar levels—the result of insulin doing its job too well—can trigger food cravings, which in turn lead to overeating and weight gain.

That's why normalizing blood sugar and insulin levels will encourage the breakdown of stored fat and keep food cravings in check,

which in turn can help curb overeating. Normal blood sugar levels can also eliminate the fatigue that may be preventing you from getting regular exercise yet prompting you to eat another cookie (and another) at 3 P.M.

It's also important to note that the foods we eat have different and significant effects on blood sugar and the subsequent release of insulin, says Alan H. Wayler, PhD, executive director of Green Mountain at Fox Run, a women's fitness and weight-loss retreat in Ludlow, Vermont. Chronic stress, inadequate sleep, and an inactive lifestyle can also cause insulin resistance and contribute to weight gain.

Not surprisingly, insulin resistance, a precursor to diabetes, is strongly linked to overweight and obesity. And the heavier you are, the more likely you are to have it.

On the positive side, you can improve your body's ability to use insulin with the right diet, adequate sleep, stress control, and physical activity.

It Could Be the Road to Diabetes

High-normal blood sugar is just one precarious step away from full-blown type 2 diabetes. If you have high-normal blood sugar, your risk of developing diabetes is raised by 50 percent within 10 years. These health dangers are too often downplayed, if they're mentioned at all.

"I call prediabetes [another term for high-normal blood sugar] the Rodney Dan-

DIABETES: ARE YOU AT RISK?

Experts recommend that adults and overweight children with any of the risk factors below have their blood sugar levels tested. If the test is normal, it should be repeated every 3 years; if the results are not normal, retest as your doctor advises (usually every 1 to 2 years).

- Family history of type 2 diabetes
- Overweight
- History of diabetes during pregnancy (gestational diabetes) or having a baby weighing 9 pounds or more at birth
- Low HDL (good) cholesterol level (below 50 for women, below 40 for men), high total cholesterol (above 200), or triglycerides above 150
- High blood pressure (above 130/85)
- Age over 45
- Inactive lifestyle
- African-American, Latino, Asian, Native American, or Pacific Island ethnicity

gerfield of human diseases. It gets no respect," says John Buse, MD, PhD, certified diabetes educator, associate professor of medicine at the University of North Carolina School of Medicine in Chapel Hill, and director of the university's diabetes care center.

The Big Belly Connection

Grab a tape measure and check your girth. If your waist is larger than 35 inches for women or 40 inches for men, the fat around your waist could be putting you at risk for heart disease and diabetes.

Another risk factor is your body mass index (BMI). More than one-quarter of Americans have a BMI of 30 or more, a level considered obese. As a result of this, diabetes is on the rise and is becoming more common among younger people and even kids.

Research suggests that belly fat—known as visceral fat, the kind that's packed around internal organs and is often linked to high levels of the stress hormone cortisol—may be an even more potent risk factor than weight alone. "Overweight, a high-fat diet, and visceral fat all intertwine to produce insulin resistance," says Dr. Buse.

Seeking Better Balance

Having high blood sugar is a lot like having termites in your house. Serious damage can happen well before you notice something's wrong. But when caught in time, most high blood sugar can be corrected before lasting damage occurs, says Gerard Bernstein, MD, associate clinical professor at Albert Einstein College of Medicine in New York City. While it's not always possible to prevent high blood sugar, there's much you can do to lower your risk.

"Our research shows that many blood sugar problems can be controlled through lifestyle factors such as diet and exercise, especially if people act early," says David M. Nathan, MD, director of the diabetes center at Massachusetts General Hospital in Boston and chairman of the National Institutes of Health Diabetes Prevention Program (DPP).

The DPP—a huge clinical study that looked at the effects of diet and exercise, medication, or a placebo in 3,234 people with high-normal blood sugar—showed how powerful lifestyle changes can be. Not only did diet and exercise prevent the development of diabetes by 58 percent, they actually were more effective than the study medication, which prevented diabetes by 31 percent!

Seek the Right Carbohydrates

One of the best things we can do to regulate blood sugar is to eat whole carbs, instead of processed carbs.

When sugars from food enter the bloodstream, the pancreas responds by pumping out more insulin. How much insulin gets made depends on the food we eat.

Fat and proteins typically cause a slow, gradual rise in blood sugar and a correspondingly slow release of insulin.

Carbohydrates raise blood sugar most

quickly, but how quickly depends on what kind of carbohydrates are eaten. Unrefined carbohydrates, found in natural foods like legumes, starchy vegetables, and whole grains, are higher in fiber, which slows the release of sugar into the bloodstream, and therefore insulin rises more gradually.

Refined carbohydrates, found in processed foods like white bread, pasta, crackers, and boxed baked goods, typically contain little or no fiber and so are digested more quickly. Their simple sugars hit the bloodstream almost immediately, causing blood sugar to skyrocket and then plunge almost as quickly.

These jagged spikes and dips in blood sugar can cause cravings (usually for more refined carbohydrates), more overeating, and weight gain. It's a vicious cycle, because the more refined carbohydrates you eat, the lower your blood sugar ultimately plunges, the hungrier you get—and the more you eat.

The cure is to choose foods high in fiber and with a low glycemic index (GI). Foods with a low GI are converted to glucose more slowly and result in a slower rise in insulin and blood sugar, discouraging fat storage. And because they stay in your system longer, fiber-rich, low-GI foods promote satiety and curb your appetite.

Look to Beans to Balance Blood Sugar

One of the best ways to control blood sugar levels naturally is to consume 20 to 30 grams of fiber a day. Beans or other legumes are terrific fiber sources. Research finds that eating small quantities of beans—just ½ cup a day—helps to manage blood sugar levels. In fact, a recent study showed that people with diabetes who ate 50 grams of fiber a day—particularly the soluble kind, found in foods like apples and oatmeal—were able to control their blood sugar better than those who ate far less. So remember, give peas (and beans) a chance.

Lose Weight and Get Moving to Stop the Blood Sugar Spiral

Overweight, high blood sugar, and excess insulin form a vicious cycle, and each of these health problems makes the others worse. Once you've packed on extra pounds, that extra weight itself makes cells resist insulin even more, leading to ever-higher sugar and insulin levels in your bloodstream. These levels in turn prompt your body to pack on more pounds. The cycle goes round and round, you gain more weight, and even worse, your risk for heart disease, stroke, and full-blown type 2 diabetes rises with the numbers on your bathroom scale.

Stopping the cycle does more than slim you down: It reduces these serious health risks. In fact, losing just 7 percent of your body weight (about 12 pounds, if you now weigh 175) can cut your odds significantly. In the Finnish Diabetes Prevention study, even extremely overweight people lowered their risk of diabetes by 70 percent when they lost just 5 percent of their total weight—even if they didn't exercise. Five percent is only 8 pounds on a 150-pound person.

People in the Finnish Diabetes Prevention study were also able to slash their diabetes risk by as much as 58 percent with only 2½ hours of exercise a week (about 21 min-

utes a day), even if they didn't lose any weight. Moderate exercise (walking, biking, playing tennis) is enough to improve your odds. More exercise is even better.

Pass on the Burgers

Can't go by a burger joint without stopping? Try reminding yourself that each time you give in, you may increase your odds of developing diabetes. Women who ate red meat at least five times a week had a 29 percent higher risk than those who ate it less than once a week, according to a 37,000-woman study at Brigham and Women's Hospital in Boston. And eating processed meats such as bacon and hot dogs at least five times a week raised diabetes risk by 43 percent, compared with eating them less than once a week. Scientists suspect the culprits are the cholesterol in red meat and the additives in the processed meat.

So red meat aside, about how much fat should you aim for in your diet, and what kind? Experts recommend that less than 30 percent of your total daily calories should come from fat, and less than 10 percent from saturated fat, the kind found in meat and full-fat dairy products. Get most of your fat from olive or canola oils, or salad dressings made from them. And spread your fat servings throughout the day—a little fat helps you to absorb the fat-soluble nutrients found in vegetables and fruits.

Eat Breakfast to Beat Diabetes

When 77 men breakfasted on various cereals, blood tests revealed that those with insulin resistance (a precursor to diabetes) had elevated blood sugar and insulin levels after eating low-fiber cereal. However, their levels were normal when the fiber was a sky-high 35 grams per bowl, say University of Toronto researchers.

Pour on fat-free or 1 percent milk for added protection. The research suggests that a daily dairy serving can slash insulin resistance risk by 20 percent, thanks to its vitamin D.

"A healthy, high-fiber breakfast could cut your risk for insulin resistance by 30 to 50 percent," says Jo-Anne Rizzotto, RD, a nutritionist at the Joslin Diabetes Center in Boston. "If you need something sweet, add some berries to your high-fiber cereal."

Nosh More, Weigh Less

Forgot to eat breakfast again? If you regularly skip meals, you're encouraging weight gain. When you don't eat breakfast and lunch,

HOW COFFEE CAN HELP YOU SHAKE THE SUGAR BLUES

Pour it on. Caffeine's yummy jolt may keep you up late, but it could also lower your risk for diabetes, says a new study of 126,210 women and men.

Researchers at the Harvard School of Public Health found that big-time coffee drinkers—those who downed more than six daily cups—had a 29 to 54 percent lower risk of developing diabetes during the 18-year study.

Sipping four or five cups cut risk by about 29 percent; one to three cups per day had little effect. Decaf offered no protection. Caffeine in other forms, such as tea, soda, and chocolate, did.

Caffeine may help by boosting metabolism. And coffee, the major caffeine source in the study, also contains potassium, magnesium, and antioxidants that help cells absorb sugar.

and then you devour a huge dinner, your body produces a flood of insulin. Besides making you hungry, higher insulin levels prevent fat cells from releasing fat into the bloodstream to be picked up and burned by other tissues. Skipping meals slows your metabolism by as much as 5 percent. An empty stomach makes your brain think that your body is starving, so it turns down its calorie-burning furnace to live off its stored fat.

Try this instead: Eat small minimeals throughout the day to keep your blood sugar steady and avoid an insulin surge. Divide what you normally eat into four to six mini-meals of about 250 calories each.

Have a Spot of Tea

Common teas boost insulin activity by more than fifteenfold, according to studies conducted by the USDA. Black, green, and oolong teas—with or without caffeine—enhanced insulin activity the most. Take your tea black, however. Adding whole, fat-free, or soy milk, or a nondairy creamer, seemed to dampen the tea's beneficial effect on insulin. Sip up to five cups a day.

Getting a Handle on Hunger

Move Past Emotional Eating

Being hungry is like being in love: If you don't know if you really are, then you're probably not. Your body is naturally wired to let you know in no uncertain terms when it wants food. But there's another kind of hunger that's easy to confuse with real hunger, and it has nothing to do with food.

When we eat because we are angry, sad, bored, lonely, or tired, or because we are celebrating, grieving, or getting ready to go on another diet, we aren't eating from real hunger, but from what food and diet expert Geneen Roth calls *mind hunger*. Eating from mind hunger, when your body has no need for food, is a sure way to pack on extra pounds. And the more we respond to mind hunger, the less certain we become that we know how to feel true body hunger; we no longer trust the innate wisdom of our biology.

Mind hunger is endless, bottomless, and erratic. You pass a bakery and suddenly you have to have an éclair, even though you ate breakfast 10 minutes ago. Or you're sitting in a restaurant, and the waiter walks by with a plate of mashed potatoes. Your mind hunger tells you that you have to have those potatoes right now, even though you're in the middle of a very good meal.

If you frequently experience mind hunger, diets don't work because they don't help you to understand and resolve the reasons

23

THE FIVE D'S OF DIETING

When you catch yourself eating more than you'd like, follow the D's.

1. **Determine** what's going on.

2. **Delay** your response by figuring out what's driving your urge to eat. Is it anger? Boredom? Loneliness?

3. **Distract** yourself for at least 10 minutes; take a short walk, water a plant, or read a poem.

4. **Distance** yourself from temptation. Throw away the bag of chips. Heck, bury them in the garbage, if you have to.

5. **Decide.** If your fork is already deep in the piece of cake, take a moment to figure out how to handle the situation. Will you stop eating, or continue? It's okay to keep going, as long as you make a conscious choice to continue rather than being helplessly out of control.

you turn to food when you aren't hungry. They can't. Even when you lose weight on a diet, you haven't necessarily lost the reasons that you overate in the first place. You don't simply lose the emotional triggers for your mind hunger. They're still there, waiting for the first opportunity to come out again and make you reach for the cookies. Read on for more advice on what to do about it.

Gain Knowledge, instead of Weight

You need to get your mind hunger under control if you want to peel off those extra pounds. To accomplish this, you have to learn how to keep yourself from eating when you're not physically hungry, and to learn how to stop eating when your body has had enough.

Most of us have no idea what "enough" means. We keep taking more than enough of what we can get (food) because we believe it's impossible to get enough of what we really want—things such as love, joy, value, happiness, contentment, understanding, and friendship.

When you start eating to satisfy your physical hunger instead of your emotional needs, having enough is simply a matter of listening to your body's signals. Here are some techniques to keep in mind; they will help you listen to what your body is telling you.

Help yourself to a hunger scale. You can learn to listen to true physical hunger by rating it on a scale of one to ten. "One" is so hungry that you're ready to eat what doesn't eat you first. "Ten" is so stuffed that when you roll over, your stomach stays on the other side of the bed. "Five" is comfortable.

If you start eating at five or above on the

EATING HABITS HAVE WEIGHTY CONSEQUENCES

Are you a breakfast dodger? Do you dine out frequently? How often do you nibble and graze?

"Understanding your eating patterns can tell you a lot about your chances of gaining weight," says researcher Yunsheng Ma, PhD, of the University of Massachusetts Medical School. Here's what he found in a new study surveying nearly 500 people about their eating habits.

- Breakfast skippers are 4½ times more likely to be overweight. Missing your morning meal causes blood sugar to dip, leaving you overly hungry and quadrupling your chance of overeating.
- Restaurant regulars (for breakfast or dinner) are twice as likely to gain weight. Foods eaten away from home tend to be higher in calories and fat and lower in fiber. Big servings encourage overeating.
- Lunch buyers are 30 to 60 percent less likely to pack on pounds. This exception to the "dine out, get dumpy" rule may be explained by the wider variety of healthy options available at lunch than at other times of the day.
- Eating four or more meals a day cuts your obesity risk by 45 percent, even when you eat the same number of calories. Eating one, two, or three big meals a day prompts your insulin levels to spike, triggering your body to store more of the food you eat as fat. The moral of the story: Divide your meals, conquer your weight.

hunger scale, you're eating from mind hunger, not body hunger. But if you start at two or three and ask your body what it wants to eat (which is different from what you think you should eat), you're eating from true, physical hunger.

Tune in to true hunger clues. When you start using the hunger scale, you may notice that you experience different sensations during each phase of hunger. For example, at three or four, you might feel cranky or spacey. At two—when you're really hungry—you'll probably feel empty and hollow.

Paying close attention to these clues will help you know when it's time to eat. It's really best not to wait until your hunger is at one, when you get so hungry that you will eat anything instead of making a healthful choice.

Aligning Your Eyes and Your Stomach

To know when we're full, most of us normally rely on external cues: an empty plate, the end of a TV show, or the bottom of the bag. But without the sense of sight, you are forced to rely on internal signals of satisfaction from your stomach and brain. So, taking visual cues out of the picture may work in your weight-loss favor. In fact, Swedish researchers found that subjects ate 22 percent less food when they were blindfolded, but they felt just as full as usual.

Short of blindfolding yourself, here are some practical ways to tune in to your body's hunger cues and eat less.

Serve individual courses. Eat your salad first, then have your entrée. Leave the extras on the stove and put only the food you are eating on the table. This will make it less convenient to reach over and have a second helping.

Take your time. If possible, stretch out your meal so you'll recognize sooner when you've had enough. Remember, your brain needs 20 minutes to get the "I'm full" message from your stomach.

Close your eyes (for the first few bites). Taste what you're eating. Pay full attention to the pleasures of eating.

Stopping the Cycle for Good: The Food/Stress Link

Even if you're not living in a construction zone or lost in a boxwood thicket, we know there is stress in your life. Learn to tone it

THINK YOURSELF SLIM

Your brain's wiring can sabotage your waistline. Outwit it with these three techniques.

Don't even have a bite. Tasting foods you crave affects your brain the same way that thinking about cocaine affects an addict's brain, according to researchers at Brookhaven National Laboratory. Brain scans done on 12 people while they sampled their favorite foods, such as cinnamon buns and lasagna, showed that brain activity jumped by 24 percent, mostly in the same areas activated when addicts think about drugs. The risk: a calorie overdose.

Limit variety. Call it the smorgasbord effect. If you're offered too many choices, you're more likely to overeat, according to new research that was conducted at the Universities of Pennsylvania and Illinois. Limit different foods on your plate to two at a time.

Treat your other senses. Fatty foods cause cravings because they stimulate your brain's pleasure centers, University of Oxford researchers found. By putting 12 people in a brain scanner and feeding them different foods by tube, they discovered that the brain reacts to the feel of fat in the mouth the same way that the nose and skin react to pleasant stimulation. So try a sensual caress or a spritz of your favorite cologne instead of the Godiva.

IS ANGER MAKING YOU FAT?

Hostility is fattening, say Duke University scientists, who found that people who stayed angry throughout young adulthood and middle age, or who became more angry over the years, were more likely to eat a high-fat diet, avoid exercise, and be overweight.

Are you headed for mad fat? Answer yes or no to these three questions.

1. Do you often find yourself annoyed at the incompetence of others?

2. Do little things, such as long traffic lights, get under your skin every day?

3. If you do get angry, do you usually blast the person who made you angry?

If you answered yes to even one question, you may have the kind of chronic anger that can torpedo your efforts to maintain, or attain, a healthy weight, says study author and anger expert Redford Williams, MD.

The fix? Evaporate hostility in a maddening situation by asking yourself: Is it important? If not, distract yourself. Is it worth taking action to change the situation that's making me angry? If not, can I accept it?

down, tune it out, and deal with what's left of it constructively, and research suggests that you will have a better handle on your overeating.

Pennsylvania State University research found that women who are less able to cope with stress—shown by blood pressure and heart rate elevations—ate twice as many fatty snacks as stress-resistant women did, even after the stress stopped (in this case, 25 minutes of periodic jackhammer-level noise and an unsolvable maze).

And you are not the only family member whose waistline may benefit from a more relaxed approach. A British study of 4,320 eleven- and twelve-year-olds found that those most harried by homework, overbooked schedules, social fears, or family worries were more likely to snack and skip breakfast. They also ate fewer fruits and vegetables.

Can the distractions; make your meal the main deal. Life is hectic. You're busy and overwhelmed; you're at your desk powering down a sandwich while answering e-mail and screening phone calls. You think you're saving time, being more efficient. Maybe so, but this style of eating is making you fat.

In a French study, 48 women ate identical lunches once a week for 4 weeks. At the two lunches during which they watched TV or listened to a story, they ate 11 percent more calories than they did at the other lunches. Focusing on nothing but food while eating can help you to know when you've had enough.

So sweep out the distractions at mealtime. When you can, make the time to sit down with your mate, your family, or just your own good company and really experience the joy

QUICK TIP

Trust your hungers: Rest when you are tired, ask for love when you need it, and eat when you're hungry.

of good food. Engage both your mind and your body. If you miss the entire meal by talking on the phone or watching television, you'll finish eating and feel as if you didn't get enough.

Making and enjoying food every day that is tasty, easy, and that fits into your diet will keep you satisfied and help you avoid mindless munching. That's where our recipes come in.

Exile no food. According to Dr. Lisa Sanders in *The Perfect Fit Diet,* in order for a diet to succeed and to outsmart the forces that help us put on weight and make it hard to lose, there can be no forbidden foods.

All foods are allowed, but you have to plan for them. Too many people simply decide to say "no" to a food they love but believe has contributed to their inability to control their weight. They decide that this food—say, a treat that is sweet or salty, filled with sugar or fat or both—may never be eaten again.

If you are going to incorporate a new way of eating into your life, you have to figure out some way to make peace with the foods you love and feel you shouldn't eat. Make room in your calorie count or diet, plan your treats, and enjoy every single bite.

When a food is no longer "forbidden," it might just become a food that you no longer crave. Often, the very fact that certain foods are forbidden is what makes them so attractive: Don't we always want what we can't have? Try giving yourself permission to enjoy a food, and you might just take the curse off it.

Putting It All Together

How to Eat Well—Forever

In the preceding chapters, you learned why you overeat, determined your perfect food plan, and got a heads-up on watching your blood sugar. Now it's time to talk about what you *should* eat for optimum health, weight loss, and, most importantly, pleasure. Pull up a plate.

Keep the Focus on Fiber

Fiber is one of your best allies in the war for weight loss and good health. It fills you up, and it keeps you feeling fuller and more satisfied for longer. As we read in the previous chapter, fiber can also help to regulate spikes in blood sugar, keeping diabetes at bay. According to James Anderson, MD, a professor

of medicine and clinical nutrition at the University of Kentucky, fiber is emerging as both a preventive and a treatment for diseases such as diabetes and obesity. Fiber can also work to lower blood cholesterol, and it might prevent colon cancer. Pass the bran, please.

Aim for 25 to 30 grams of fiber a day. Remember to drink plenty of water, and if you're new to fiber, build up your intake slowly so you won't suffer the bloat.

Soluble vs. Insoluble Fiber: Which Matters Most?

First off, take note: Both types matter. Soluble and insoluble fiber each have different and important functions. As long as you eat at least 25 grams of fiber a day, you'll get

BREAKFAST EATERS STAY SLIMMER JUST BY EATING

A Harvard Medical School study found that breakfast eaters have half the risk of obesity and insulin resistance (a precursor to diabetes) that breakfast skippers do.

"When we eat, our body experiences the 'thermic effect,' which means we burn calories just by digesting and absorbing our food," says Lona Sandon, RD, assistant professor at the University of Texas Southwestern Medical Center at Dallas. "If you get up at 7 A.M., skip breakfast, and don't eat your first meal until noon, that's 5 hours during which your calorie burn has slowed down," Sandon explains.

Furthermore, studies show that regular breakfast eaters eat less fat and fewer calorie-dense foods all day. Consuming most of your calories early in the day means you're less likely to overeat or snack in the evening.

enough of both kinds, says Greg Hottinger, MPH, RD, staff nutritionist for the Duke Center for Integrative Medicine in Durham, North Carolina.

Soluble fiber retains water and turns into a gel during digestion. It lowers cholesterol and slows the absorption of food from the digestive tract, thereby controlling blood sugar levels. Good sources are beans, oat bran, oatmeal, fruits, and many vegetables.

Insoluble fiber (Grandma would call it "roughage") passes through the intestinal tract without breaking down. It helps maintain bowel regularity and possibly reduces colon cancer risk by limiting the time the intestinal lining is exposed to toxins. Good sources are whole grain products, wheat bran, and vegetables.

How to Get Fiber in Every Meal

Eating the recommended 25 to 35 grams a day isn't as daunting as it may sound if you start slowly and heed the following advice.

Start with breakfast. Fitting in fiber at breakfast is a snap. Fiber is found in abundance in whole grain cereals and whole grain breads. Add some fat-free or low-fat milk, plus berries, raisins, or sliced banana, and you can be halfway to your daily fiber goal. So cruise the cereal aisle and read the labels. You'll find plenty of good options to choose from.

Lunch and snacks: Build some bread into the menu. Bread is not your enemy. In fact, you can slash your odds for extra pounds in half if you eat the whole grain, high-fiber version. In a Harvard study of 74,000 women, those who ate more than two daily servings of whole grains were 49 percent less likely to be overweight than

SPECIAL NEWS FOR PASTA LOVERS

Pasta is one of America's favorite supper dishes, but it's high in carbs and fairly low in fiber. To make it healthier, switch over to whole grain pasta. If you've tried that, but you find most whole-grain pastas too strong in flavor, check out the tasty new, higher-fiber pasta from Barilla (see page 170).

It's also easy to fiber up your regular pasta and marinara sauce. Instead of adding high-fat sausage or ground beef, stir in cooked high-fiber vegetables, such as green peas, Swiss chard, broccoli or broccoli rabe, or some canned beans. Also, see our quick recipes below. Each uses 2 cups of plain, jarred marinara sauce and ½ pound of pasta to serve 4 people.

Pasta Pepperonata. While the pasta (use ziti or bow-ties) is cooking, heat 2 tablespoons of olive oil in a large nonstick skillet and sauté 1 sliced large onion and 3 slivered garlic cloves until tender. Cut 2 red bell peppers into thin strips, and add them to the skillet. Continue cooking, stirring often, until the peppers are tender. Stir in the marinara sauce and 1 cup of drained, canned cannellini beans. Heat through. Toss with the drained pasta.

Broccoli-Ceci Pasta. When the pasta (penne, medium shells, or rigatoni) has about 6 more minutes to cook, stir a package of frozen chopped broccoli into the boiling water. Cook together until the pasta and broccoli are tender. Then stir in a drained can of chickpeas and heat through. Drain the pasta, veggies, and chickpeas, and toss with the marinara sauce.

those who noshed on the virtually fiberless white stuff.

If you're having a sandwich for lunch, make it on whole wheat instead of white or rye and you'll get up to 2 grams of fiber per slice. Check the label before you buy. The first ingredient should be whole wheat flour, not just wheat flour, which is plain old white flour. Also look for whole wheat flour tortillas, whole wheat pitas, and whole wheat rolls for sandwiches or wraps. For snacking, choose whole grain crackers, especially the baked ones, without trans fats.

Slather on the spreadables. Two zesty, fiber-full sandwich spreads are mashed avocado with lime or salsa, and hummus. Spread on pitas or crusty whole grain bread, and pile on spinach leaves, tomato, sweet onion, and cucumber slices. For more protein, add crumbled feta or sliced hard-cooked egg.

Another way to boost fiber at lunch is with a hearty serving of crisp, raw veggies, such as baby carrots, bell peppers, broccoli florets, or green beans. Veggies are great for snacking, too. If you want some protein with your snack, have some yogurt dip, a small container of low-fat cottage cheese, or some string cheese.

Savor your salad days. Lunching at your desk? Dig into a crispy green side salad fibered-up with shredded red cabbage, carrots, avocado, and chickpeas or black beans. Make it a main dish with a heartier serving of beans, cooked veggies (try last night's leftovers), almonds, and a hard-cooked egg, boiled shrimp, or lean chicken or beef.

Fruit all around. Finish your lunch with a piece of fruit, or tote some for a snack. Dried fruit is portable and fiber-full: 2 dried

figs have 4.6 grams of fiber, 5 dates have 3.1 grams, ¼ cup of dark raisins pack 2 grams of fiber, and 3 medium dried plums (prunes) have 1.7 grams. Munch on a few almonds for even more delicious fiber.

On the fresh side, one apple has 3.7 grams of fiber, an orange has 3.1 grams, and a banana weighs in with a respectable 2.8 grams.

Dinner: Make the most of it. Begin the meal with a robust (but lean) bean or vegetable-barley soup, or serve bigger portions of soup for the main event for a big fiber kick. Toss a salad of colorful mixed greens, lots of veggies, and beans, and start (or finish) supper in style with sliced fresh fruit such as pineapple, mango, kiwifruit, or berries.

An easy way to get more fiber at dinner is

to fill half your plate with vegetables, as long as they're not swimming in butter or cream or covered in cheese and crumbs. Some favorite fiber-packed veggies are green peas, baked sweet or russet potatoes (with the skin), winter squash, broccoli, dark leafy greens, corn, green beans, and carrots. A serving is generally ½ cup, and you should aim for 6 servings a day, or 3 cups, along with 2 cups of fruit. See page 34 for more about vegetable servings.

Go with great grains. Serve brown rice instead of white, whole wheat couscous (really a pasta), quinoa, bulgur, and barley to increase your fiber intake. Brown rice is available precooked in heat-and-serve packets, which makes it super easy if you're pressed for time. Whole wheat couscous cooks in about 10 minutes; quinoa and bulgur both cook in about 15 minutes. If you add green peas or wilted greens, or stir in sautéed onion and peppers, or some canned beans, you can boost the fiber content even more.

Include All the Building Blocks of a Healthful Diet

While fiber is hands-down the key ingredient to avoiding hunger while losing weight, there are a lot of other important nutrients you should pay attention to, as well. Read on for important advice on how to make sure you get everything your body needs to lose the weight you want to lose.

Carbs—They're a Good Thing

Carbohydrates are found in a great variety of foods; they're in all the sugars and all the starches that we consume. They are our main source of energy, and like all foods, they are broken down into glucose (a type of sugar) during digestion. But carbohydrates convert into blood sugar much more quickly than fats and protein do. Unrefined, whole carbs take longer to digest and convert to blood sugar than refined carbs do. Put simply, they are a better-quality fuel. Carbohydrates are mostly plant-based, except for the carbs found in dairy products.

We've placed a lot of emphasis on fiber, but we want you to understand that most of the foods that are high in fiber are also high in carbohydrates. These carbs are good carbs; you'll find them in unrefined, whole grain breads, grains, and cereals, and in legumes, fruits, and vegetables.

These good, high-fiber carbs should not be shunned. Even if you're counting carbohydrates, whole carbs should make up part of your daily diet. They are an essential part of healthful eating, and they help to fight disease and obesity.

Lean Proteins Make a Lean Body

An amino acid that is found in protein is essential for developing lean muscle mass and regulating the hormones that control your appetite and help you burn calories. The amount you need is

A BETTER SNACK

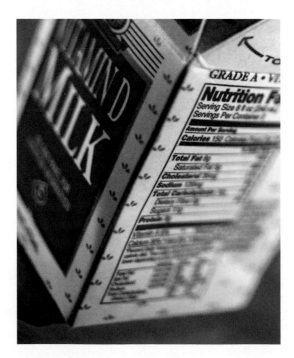

If you snack on produce three times each day instead of on soda and chips, you can expect to lose about 1 pound per week. A produce-packed diet also arms your body against heart disease, diabetes, and possibly some cancers, and it may keep your bones strong by helping them retain calcium.

specific: two 2- to 3-ounce servings of lean protein each day. Lean proteins include skinless chicken; lean cuts of beef, pork, and lamb; fish; and low-fat dairy products.

Recent studies support protein's slimming benefits: Researchers at the University of Illinois at Urbana-Champaign found that women who ate more protein but took in the same number of calories lost more weight and retained more lean body mass than those on a lower-protein diet. Here's the catch: Eating larger amounts of protein than is recommended backfires, big time. Too much won't allow your body to use protein's amino acids efficiently, and if that big steak dinner (some restaurant cuts are 32 ounces!) pushes you over your calorie count for the day, that excess protein is more likely to be stored as extra fat than as muscle. You need only 6 ounces a day.

Dairy Is In

Eating three servings of fat-free or low-fat dairy products a day is one of the best things

that you can do for your bones and your belly. University of Tennessee researchers suggest that the calcium in dairy foods increases the breakdown of fat—especially harmful belly fat—while suppressing fat storage. So make that fat-free yogurt all around.

Eat More Veggies

The revised 2005 Dietary Guidelines for Americans have a new goal for all of us: Eat more vegetables and fruits. At every meal, one half of your plate should be filled with vegetables and fruit. This half-plate guideline makes it easy to reach a daily total of 5 cups combined—that's 3 cups of vegetables and 2 cups of fruit.

In your daily servings, include the following "potent" produce, preferably in whole, not juice, form. Choose something red (tomatoes), something deep green (kale or broccoli), something orange (carrots or squash), or something citrus (grapefruit or oranges).

Salads and Soups

SALADS

SOUPS

177 Calories

Toasted Almond Chicken Salad

—Linda Chaput, Rutherglen, Ontario, Canada

Prep time: 20 minutes
Chill time: 1 hour

- 3 small chicken breast halves
- 3 ribs celery, sliced
- 1 bunch chives, finely chopped
- ½ cup low-fat plain yogurt
- ¼ cup light sour cream
- 1½ teaspoons dried tarragon
- 2 tablespoons slivered almonds, toasted
  Salt
  Ground black pepper
- 1 bag (10 ounces) mixed greens

Coat a nonstick skillet with cooking spray and place over medium-high heat. When it's hot, add the chicken and cook for 4 minutes per side, or until the juices run clear. Remove the chicken from the heat and let it rest for at least 10 minutes. When they're cool enough to handle, chop the chicken breasts into small pieces.

In a large bowl, combine the chicken, celery, chives, yogurt, sour cream, and tarragon. Mix lightly.

Cover and refrigerate for at least 1 hour, or up to 24 hours. Add the almonds, and salt and pepper to taste. Serve on a bed of greens.

Makes 4 servings

Per serving: *177 calories, 25 g protein, 8 g carbohydrate, 5 g fat, 58 mg cholesterol, 144 mg sodium, 3 g fiber*

Diet Exchanges: *0 milk, 1 vegetable, 0 fruit, 0 bread, 3 meat, 1 fat*

½ Carb Choice

Kitchen Tip

To toast the almonds, place them in a dry skillet over medium-low heat, shaking the pan often, until the almonds are fragrant and slightly browned (2 to 3 minutes). Remove from the heat and stir until the almonds cool slightly and emit a pronounced toasted aroma.

Blue Ridge Chopped Salad

270 Calories

—Vikki Baird, Atlanta, Georgia

"It is a light meal in itself, full of different flavors."

Prep time: 15 minutes
Cook time: 6 minutes

- 3 **chicken breasts (6 ounces each)**
- ½ **head iceberg lettuce, chopped**
- 1 **head romaine lettuce, chopped**
- 3 **medium tomatoes, chopped**
- ½ **cup reduced-fat ranch dressing**
- ½ **cup reduced-sodium crumbled blue cheese**
- 6 **slices cooked bacon, finely chopped**

Preheat the broiler. Coat a broiler pan with cooking spray. Place the chicken on the pan and cook on high for 3 minutes per side, or until the chicken is no longer pink in the center. When the chicken is cool enough to handle, chop it into small pieces. Set aside.

Combine the lettuce and tomatoes in a medium bowl. Toss with the dressing. Arrange each serving on a plate and top with the blue cheese, bacon, and chicken.

Makes 6 servings

Per serving: *270 calories, 28 g protein, 11 g carbohydrate, 13 g fat, 75 mg cholesterol, 610 mg sodium, 2 g fiber*

Diet Exchanges: *0 milk, 1½ vegetable, 0 fruit, ½ bread, 4 meat, 2 fat*

1 Carb Choice

SECRETS OF WEIGHT-LOSS WINNERS

• Find a neighbor who is as interested in regular walking as you are. It's true that with a walking partner, the motivation to get up and go continues every day!

—Gloria Finley, Ann Arbor, Michigan

• Schedule your workouts with a friend and you are less likely to back out than if you hadn't made a commitment to someone else.

—Sasha Moulton, Halifax, Nova Scotia

• Buy a cheap handheld game to use in the evenings and when you're tempted to eat. I also try to have other "hand" work nearby if I'm watching TV. It keeps me from making unnecessary trips to the kitchen.

—Claudia Stanley, Windham, Maine

• Hang up the item of clothing that you would like to be able to get into someplace where you will see it every day.

—Debi Engle, Eufaula, Oklahoma

My Big Fat Greek-Style Chicken Salad

—Lillian Julow, Gainesville, Florida

308 Calories

"Replacing mayonnaise or bottled dressings with yogurt made a big difference in my own battle of the bulge. And I love using fresh herbs such as oregano to give my meals a big flavor boost."

Prep time: 15 minutes
Microwave time: 15 seconds

DRESSING

¾ cup plain low-fat yogurt
2 tablespoons lemon juice
1 tablespoon red wine vinegar
2 teaspoons oregano, finely chopped
2 small garlic cloves, minced
  Salt
  Ground black pepper

SALAD

1 bag (5 ounces) salad greens
2 cooked rotisserie chicken breasts, skinned and cut into chunks
1 pint grape tomatoes, halved
3 Kirby cucumbers, peeled and sliced
1 cup kalamata olives, sliced
½ small red onion, thinly sliced
½ cup feta cheese, crumbled
4 whole wheat pitas (8" each)

To make the dressing: In a small bowl, combine the yogurt, lemon juice, vinegar, oregano, and garlic. Season to taste with salt and pepper. Set aside.

To make the salad: In a large bowl, combine the salad greens, chicken, tomatoes, cucumbers, olives, onion, and feta. Add the dressing and toss gently to combine.

Wrap the pitas in a paper towel, warm them in a microwave for 15 to 20 seconds, and serve with the salad.

Makes 6 servings

Per serving: *308 calories, 19 g protein, 39 g carbohydrate, 9 g fat, 37 mg cholesterol, 701 mg sodium, 6 g fiber*

Diet Exchanges: *0 milk, 1 vegetable, 0 fruit, 2 bread, 2 meat, 1 fat*

2½ Carb Choices

Taco Salad

500 Calories

—Jennifer Lawlor, Guelph, Ontario, Canada

Prep time: 10 minutes
Cook time: 7 minutes

   1 **pound 85% lean ground beef**
   1 **package (¾ ounce) taco seasoning**
   ¼ **cup water**
   1 **head romaine lettuce, chopped**
   1 **can (11 ounces) corn, drained**
   2 **tomatoes, chopped**
   1 **small jar (8 ounces) low-fat Catalina salad dressing**
   1 **package (8 ounces) baked tortilla chips, crushed**

Coat a large, nonstick skillet with cooking spray and place it over medium-high heat. Add the beef and cook for 5 minutes, or until it's browned. Drain any accumulated fat and add the taco seasoning and water. Stir until the mixture begins to thicken. Remove from the heat.

In a large bowl, combine the lettuce, corn, tomatoes, and dressing. Toss gently to coat. Top with the meat and the chips just before serving.

Makes 8 servings

Per serving: *500 calories, 20 g protein, 54 g carbohydrate, 23 g fat, 53 mg cholesterol, 1202 mg sodium, 4 g fiber*

Diet Exchanges: *0 milk, 1 vegetable, 0 fruit, 3 bread, 2 meat, 3 fat*

3½ Carb Choices

Pineapple Dinner Salad

—Nancy Sheehan, Spencer, Massachusetts

350 Calories

"This is an absolutely delicious and satisfying meal. Having it to look forward to helps stave off temptation throughout the day, and I find the pineapple helps quiet my sweet tooth!"

Prep time: 15 minutes
Microwave time: 5 minutes

2 skinless, boneless chicken breasts (6 ounces each)

⅓ cup reduced-fat mayonnaise

2 tablespoons honey

⅓ cup reduced-fat sour cream

2 teaspoons mustard

1 pineapple, chopped

1 Red Delicious apple, chopped

1 small cucumber, halved and sliced

1 avocado, chopped

1 red bell pepper, cut into ½" pieces

Place the chicken on a microwavable plate and microwave on medium for 3 to 5 minutes, turning once, until the chicken is no longer pink in the center and is cooked through. Let the chicken stand until it's cool enough to handle, and then cut it into strips. Set aside.

In a small bowl, combine the mayonnaise, honey, sour cream, and mustard. Set aside.

In a medium bowl, combine the pineapple, apple, cucumber, avocado, pepper, and chicken strips. Serve with the dressing on the side.

Makes 4 servings

Per serving: *350 calories, 23 g protein, 40 g carbohydrates, 13 g fat, 55 mg cholesterol, 7 g fiber, 270 mg sodium, 7 g fiber*

Diet Exchanges: *0 milk, 1 vegetable, 1½ fruit, 1 bread, 3 meat, 2½ fat*

3 Carb Choices

Sweet and Spicy Warm Chicken Salad

—Maris Trzeciak, New Kensington, Pennsylvania

170 Calories

"It's easy and you can add or delete the veggies you like or put in fat-free cheeses."

Prep time: 10 minutes
Cook time: 6 minutes

- 2 chicken breast halves, sliced
- 1 small onion, diced
- 1 jalapeño chile pepper, sliced (wear plastic gloves when handling)
- 1 can (6½ ounces) sliced mushrooms, drained
- 1 bag (1 pound) baby spinach
- 1 cucumber, sliced
- ½ cup dried orange-flavored cranberries
- ½ cup fat-free croutons
  Salt
  Ground black pepper
- ½ cup fat-free raspberry pecan salad dressing

Coat a large nonstick saucepan with cooking spray. Add the chicken and cook on medium-high heat for 3 minutes. Remove and keep warm. Add the onion, jalapeño, and mushrooms. Cook for 3 minutes, or until brown. Mix with the chicken.

In a large bowl, combine the chicken mixture with the spinach, cucumber, cranberries, croutons, and salt and pepper to taste. Add the dressing and toss gently to combine. Serve immediately.

Makes 6 servings

Per serving: *170 calories, 13 g protein, 29 g carbohydrate, 2 g fat, 23 mg cholesterol, 328 mg sodium, 6 g fiber*

Diet Exchanges: *0 milk, 2 vegetable, ½ fruit, ½ bread, 1½ meat, 0 fat*

2 Carb Choices

It Worked for Me!

Tessie Konya

VITAL STATS

Weight lost: 50 pounds

Time to goal: 1 year

Greatest challenge: Resurrecting an exercise habit that had fallen away

As a young woman, Tessie Konya had a strong, athletic figure. During her transition to adulthood, though, life stresses and fewer opportunities to be active attracted excess pounds. For Tessie, getting back into exercise was the hidden key to weight loss. And it didn't call for competitive sports: All she needed was a simple (but consistent) daily walk.

"Growing up, I was never quite thin, but more big-boned. I started to gain weight in college, and was very heavy by the time I decided—by accident, really—to try rowing. I was out of shape, but made the team because of my height (I'm 5'10", which is an asset to a rowing crew). Rowing 6 days a week allowed me to lose some weight and added muscle.

"I finished school and rowing, but I was still eating as if I was working out 6 days a week. By 1995, I was living in Cincinnati and was at a point when I decided to stop weighing myself—the scale read 225 and I wore a size 18.

"I was 7 months pregnant when circum-stances led me to move to New Jersey. Three months after the birth of my son, I remembered there was a boat club at the local high school, and I asked if there was any rowing going on in the area. I have to say, getting back into rowing was what restored my sanity. But what helped me drop the pounds were the daily walks I took with my mother. Every morning we would take Andrew out in his stroller and walk a half hour to the local bagel shop, talking heart-to-heart the whole way. We'd drink our coffee and make our way back, my mom listening to my problems. The walks never even got me out of breath, but I realized the consistency was what I needed more than athletic intensity. The pounds started to fall off.

"My son is now a busy 5-year-old and I try to be involved in his activities as much as possible. Staying active with family tae kwon do classes, skating lessons, and by coaching my son's soccer team has helped me keep the weight off for 4 years now, even though I hardly even feel like I am exercising."

Tuna Salad

—Suzanne Denys, Alsip, Illinois

*"Try this low-fat salad with high-fiber crackers.
The combination fills you up, so you eat less and are satisfied longer."*

191
Calories

Prep time: 10 minutes

2 cans (6 ounces each) albacore tuna, drained

¼ cup black olives, pitted and halved

1 tablespoon chopped parsley

1 plum tomato, finely chopped

1 Kosher dill pickle, finely chopped (optional)

2 tablespoons olive oil

Ground black pepper

4 leaves Boston lettuce

In a large bowl, combine the tuna, olives, parsley, tomato, and pickle, if using. Add the oil and pepper to taste, and mix gently to combine. Arrange the lettuce leaves on each plate and top with the tuna mixture.

Makes 4 servings

Per serving: *191 calories, 20 g protein, 2 g carbohydrate, 11 g fat, 36 mg cholesterol, 402 mg sodium, 0 g fiber*

Diet Exchanges: *0 milk, 0 vegetable, 0 fruit, 0 bread, 3 meat, 2 fat*

0 Carb Choice

Quick Pasta Salad

—Jill Bryant, Greenwood, South Carolina

"The whole wheat pasta tastes the same as the regular, and it helps me to eat healthier. I'm also eating more vegetables, because I experiment with different ones in my pasta."

112 Calories

Prep time: 10 minutes
Cook time: 10 minutes

1½ **cups whole wheat rotini**
1 **plum tomato, finely chopped**
½ **cucumber, sliced, halved lengthwise, and seeded**
2 **tablespoons crumbled feta cheese**
2 **tablespoons light Italian dressing**

Cook the pasta according to the package directions. Drain it, rinse it in cold water, and drain it again.

In a large bowl, combine the pasta with the tomato and cucumber. Gently fold in the feta and toss with the dressing to coat. Serve at room temperature or refrigerate for 30 minutes before serving.

Makes 4 servings

Per serving: *112 calories, 4 g protein, 19 g carbohydrate, 2 g fat, 4 mg cholesterol, 112 mg sodium, 1 g fiber*

Diet Exchanges: *0 milk, ½ vegetable, 0 fruit, 1 bread, 0 meat, ½ fat*

1 Carb Choice

HEIRLOOM TOMATOES

The term "heirloom tomatoes" refers not to one type of tomato, but to a collection of old-fashioned varieties beloved by gardeners. Heirlooms are known for their outstanding flavor, bumpy shapes, poetic names, and short, fragile shelf lives. Many heirloom tomatoes seemed slated for extinction. Luckily they've been preserved through organizations such as Seed Savers and prescient gardeners

who kept seeds from their favorite tomatoes and passed those seeds on.

Due to the popularity of heirloom varieties at farm markets and better restaurants, top chefs started working with farmers to grow them commercially. Today, about a dozen heirlooms are commonly sold, distributed by Melissa's. But the best of the heirlooms will always be found from May to September, says company spokesperson Robert Schueller.

The list on the next page, prepared with help from Mr. Schueller, describes a few of the more readily available types of heirlooms. They're a joy to grow in your garden, but if you don't have a garden or a green thumb, look for them at farm markets or where specialty produce is sold.

Black Crimson. A Russian heirloom with solid meat and a hearty flavor. When sliced, a beautiful magenta and green interior is revealed.

Black Prince Tomato. Don't let its dark appearance stop you from sampling this wonderfully sweet and nutty tomato. The red flesh is surprisingly thick, and this heirloom makes a great substitute for regular tomatoes.

Brandywine. An Amish heirloom dating to 1885, this wine-colored beefsteak is a favorite for its exceptionally sweet flavor.

Great White. This unusual heirloom variety is said to have been grown at Monticello. It's very meaty with few seeds—a real showstopper for your table.

Green Zebra Tomato. A small heirloom, yellowish green in color when ripe. Very appropriately named, this tomato is naturally striped with assorted green markings.

Golden Jubilee. A large heirloom with a bright yellow color. Its thick, meaty, yellow flesh is very mild in flavor, with low acidity.

Marvel Stripe. Preserved through five generations of a family in Oxaca, Mexico, this large beefsteak-style tomato is special. It's stunning to look at, with unique yellow and red stripes, and it has a mildly sweet flavor.

Pineapple. Originating in the Carolinas, this heirloom beefsteak is a gorgeous bi-color (red-yellow) both outside and inside. Sweet!

Purple Cherokee. An heirloom from Tennessee credited to the Cherokee Indians. It's rose red on the outside and a deep brick red inside, with a great flavor.

100 Calories

Heartthrob Salad

—Estella Haines, New Canaan, Connecticut

"This salad let me have a huge portion without the fat usually associated with salad dressings. I felt great eating it and it helped me reach my goal weight."

Prep time: 10 minutes
Chill time: 2 hours

4 plum tomatoes, chopped
2 tablespoons finely chopped fresh parsley
6 kalamata olives, pitted and chopped
1 tablespoon white wine vinegar
1 teaspoon Dijon mustard
½ teaspoon olive oil
⅛ teaspoon salt
⅛ teaspoon freshly ground pepper
1 clove garlic, finely chopped
3 hearts of palm
1 head Bibb lettuce, thinly sliced
1 teaspoon grated Parmesan cheese

In a medium bowl, combine the tomatoes, parsley, olives, vinegar, mustard, oil, salt, pepper, and garlic.

Chop 1 of the hearts of palm, and add it to the tomato mixture. Cover and chill for 2 hours.

Slice the remaining 2 hearts of palm in half lengthwise. Arrange 2 hearts of palm halves, ¾ cup of lettuce, and ¾ cup of the chilled tomato mixture on each of 2 salad plates. Top each serving with ½ teaspoon of cheese.

Makes 2 servings

Per serving: *100 calories, 4 g protein, 11 g carbohydrate, 5 g fat, 0 mg cholesterol, 510 mg sodium, 3 g fiber*

Diet Exchanges: *0 milk, 1½ vegetable, 0 fruit, 0 bread, 0 meat, 1 fat*

1 Carb Choice

Coleslaw and Cumin Salad

—David Payne, Spokane, Washington

80 Calories

"There aren't many calories in this one."

Prep time: 15 minutes

½ head of cabbage, shredded
2 carrots, grated
1 small onion, sliced
2 tablespoons vinaigrette dressing
1 teaspoon cumin seeds

In a large bowl, mix together the cabbage, carrots, and onion. Add the vinaigrette and cumin seeds.

Makes 4 servings

Per serving: *80 calories, 2 g protein, 11 g carbohydrate, 4 g fat, 0 mg cholesterol, 95 mg sodium, 3 g fiber*

Diet Exchanges: *0 milk, 2 vegetable, 0 fruit, 0 bread, 0 meat, 1 fat*

1 Carb Choice

SECRETS OF WEIGHT-LOSS WINNERS

• Make exercise as routine as going to work, and eventually it will be a regular part of your daily activities.

—Sasha Moulton, Halifax, Nova Scotia

• Set a goal that's important to you. We are adopting a young boy from Russia, and I want to be thin when we meet him. My love for and anticipation of our new son strengthens my willpower and makes me want to exercise more.

—Elaine Sweet, Dallas, Texas

• You look as attractive as you feel. So, if you are not feeling attractive, tidy yourself up by keeping your hair clean and neat, and applying light makeup—even just mascara. If you look good, you'll feel good about yourself no matter what size you are! And if you feel good about yourself, you will want to feel even better by getting in shape as best you can.

—Joy Greenway, Campbell River, British Columbia

146 Calories

What a Salad!

—Heidi Brandariz, Branchville, New Jersey

*"I would rather have this great salad for dinner than any other diet item.
I often make it for lunch and dinner—it is just a great meal."*

**Prep time: 10 minutes
Cook time: 1 minute**

½ cup pine nuts

   Juice of 1 lemon

½ teaspoon red wine vinegar

2 tablespoons olive oil

   Salt

   Ground black pepper

1 bag (9 ounces) baby spinach

1 cup sliced red cabbage

1 cup basil, thinly sliced

½ cup pitted kalamata olives, halved

½ cup shredded Parmesan cheese

In a skillet over medium-high heat, toast the pine nuts, stirring frequently, for about 1 minute, or until they're fragrant and lightly browned. Set them aside to cool.

In a small bowl, whisk together the lemon juice, vinegar, oil, and salt and pepper to taste. Set aside.

In a large bowl, combine the spinach, cabbage, basil, and olives. Add the dressing and pine nuts, tossing gently to combine. Garnish with the Parmesan.

Makes 8 servings

Per serving: *146 calories, 4 g protein, 7 g carbohydrate, 12 g fat, 4 mg cholesterol, 215 mg sodium, 2 g fiber*

Diet Exchanges: *0 milk, 1 vegetable, 0 fruit, 0 bread, ½ meat, 2 fat*

½ Carb Choice

No-Salad-Dressing Salad

—Rosalind Rauschenberg, Blountstown, Florida

104 Calories

"This salad is so good, you do not need any salad dressing. Not even a squirt of lemon! But if you'd like, add the oil from the jar of kalamata olives. Delicious!"

Prep time: 15 minutes

  4 cups sliced Chinese cabbage
  4 cups sliced hearts of iceberg lettuce
  4 cups baby spinach
 10 kalamata olives, pitted and chopped
  1 cup mushrooms, sliced
  4 Roma tomatoes, chopped
  1 green bell pepper, chopped
  3 cloves garlic, finely chopped
  ¼ cup shredded Parmesan cheese

In a large bowl, combine the cabbage, lettuce, spinach, olives, mushrooms, tomatoes, pepper, and garlic. Sprinkle with the Parmesan cheese before serving.

Makes 4 servings

Per serving: *104 calories, 6 g protein, 12 g carbohydrate, 5 g fat, 5 mg cholesterol, 351 mg sodium, 4 g fiber*

Diet Exchanges: *0 milk, 2 vegetable, 0 fruit, 0 bread, ½ meat, 1 fat*

1 Carb Choice

Walnut Salad

147 Calories

—Andrina Goetz, Cypress, California

"To cut down on your prep time, buy prepackaged greens."

Prep time: 20 minutes

  3 cups iceberg lettuce
  3 cups Romaine lettuce
  1 cup cherry tomatoes, halved
  ¼ cup walnuts, roughly chopped
  1 cucumber, peeled and sliced into rounds
  ½ cup vinaigrette

In a large bowl, toss together the lettuces. Add the tomatoes, walnuts, and cucumber. Add the dressing, and mix gently.

Makes 6 servings

Per serving: *147 calories, 2 g protein, 6 g carbohydrate, 13 g fat, 0 mg cholesterol, 173 mg sodium, 2 g fiber*

Diet Exchanges: *0 milk, 1 vegetable, 0 fruit, 0 bread, 0 meat, 2½ fat*

½ Carb Choice

SECRETS OF WEIGHT-LOSS WINNERS

• Try to think of emotional eating as putting a piece of chocolate cake on a skinned knee. The treatment or cure doesn't fit the injury.

—Linda Lindsey, Kennesaw, Georgia

• If you miss a workout or two or three, don't get discouraged and give up completely. Tomorrow is another day, and you have the rest of your life!

—Sasha Moulton, Halifax, Nova Scotia

• Keep a pair of your "skinny jeans" hanging on a hook by your closet. Each morning, try and slip them on; you'll be motivated throughout the day to eat sensibly so that you can someday fit back into those jeans.

—Nancy Roth, Saint Joseph, Illinois

Fruity Lettuce Salad with Lemon Dressing

—Kim Flanegan, Hampton, Minnesota

138 Calories

"I received this recipe from a coworker. I've found that it is a good way to get some fruit and vegetables into my diet."

Prep time: 15 minutes

D R E S S I N G

- ¼ cup sugar
- ⅓ cup lemon juice
- 2 teaspoons finely minced onion
- 1 teaspoon Dijon mustard
- ½ teaspoon salt
- ⅓ cup olive oil
- 1 tablespoon poppy seeds

S A L A D

- 1 bag (1 pound) romaine lettuce, torn into bite-size pieces
- 3 ounces reduced-fat Swiss cheese, shredded
- ½ cup cashews, chopped
- ¼ cup sweetened dried cranberries
- 1 apple, peeled and chopped
- 1 pear, peeled and chopped
- 1 large can (15 ounces) mandarin oranges, drained

To make the dressing: In a blender, blend together the sugar, lemon juice, onion, mustard, and salt. With the blender running, slowly add the oil until the mixture's thick and smooth. Stir in the poppy seeds.

To make the salad: In a large bowl, combine the lettuce, cheese, cashews, cranberries, apple, pear, and oranges.

Add the dressing, and toss gently to coat.

Makes 14 servings

Per serving: *138 calories, 3 g protein, 15 g carbohydrate, 8 g fat, 2 mg cholesterol, 114 mg sodium, 1 g fiber*

Diet Exchanges: *0 milk, ½ vegetable, ½ fruit, ½ bread, ½ meat, 1½ fat*

1 Carb Choice

GRAPES—THEY'RE BRAIN FOOD

Make grapes a regular part of your diet, and you may survive a stroke with more of your brain cells intact. In one study of people who have had strokes, researchers found that a nutrient found in grapes (resveratrol) prevented part of the subsequent brain damage that typically accompanies brain injuries. And like red wine, red grapes are high in resveratrol, which is concentrated in their seeds and skin. So grab a bunch today; they're good for you.

Grapes are also a good source of vitamin C and antioxidants, and are low in calories, with only 90 calories per ¾ cup. They're portable and great for snacking, and they don't require further ripening or much prep work, except for rinsing, which should be done prior to munching.

This delicious salsa-salad comes from the California Table Grape Commission. It combines two very healthful fruits and tastes great served over grilled chicken or fish, or eaten all by itself.

Mango-grape salsa with cilantro and lime. Dice 2 ripe mangos, and mix with 2 cups of halved grapes, ¼ cup of minced red onion, 2 tablespoons each of chopped cilantro and lime juice, and one minced and seeded jalapeño chile pepper. Season to taste with salt and freshly ground black pepper. Makes 4 cups.

65 Calories

Tangy Citrus Salad
—Ronni Fox, Buffalo, New York

"This salad is colorful, has a wonderful blend of textures and flavors, is packed with vitamins, and tastes great. I never feel deprived. I frequently take it to parties and serve it spooned over slices of angel food cake. I never have leftovers."

Prep time: 15 minutes

3 oranges, peeled and sectioned
1 cup seedless grapes
2 kiwifruit, peeled and diced
1 cup chopped pineapple
1 mango or papaya, peeled and sliced
Juice of 1 lime
Juice of 1 lemon
½ cup fat-free sour cream
2 packets of artificial sweetener (optional)

In a large bowl, combine the oranges, grapes, kiwi, pineapple, and mango or papaya. In a small bowl, stir together the lime juice, lemon juice, sour cream, and sweetener, if using. Gently toss with the fruit.

Makes 12 servings

Per serving: *65 calories, 1 g protein, 17 g carbohydrate, 0 g fat, 1 mg cholesterol, 9 mg sodium, 3 g fiber*

Diet Exchanges: *0 milk, 0 vegetable, 1 fruit, 0 bread, 0 meat, 0 fat*

1 Carb Choice

143 Calories

Watermelon Salad

—Carol Auld, Toronto, Ontario, Canada

"We all need more greens and we all need to be eating more fresh ingredients, like watermelon. I found this salad filling and refreshing. Because it's so simple to prepare, it helped me lose weight."

Prep time: 10 minutes

1 bag (4 ounces) arugula, stems removed and roughly torn

2 cups cubed watermelon

1 package (3 ounces) feta cheese, crumbled

2 tablespoons olive oil

Ground black pepper

In a large bowl, combine the arugula, watermelon, and feta. Gently mix in the olive oil and pepper to taste.

Makes 4 servings

Per serving: *143 calories, 4 g protein, 9 g carbohydrate, 11 g fat, 19 mg cholesterol, 248 mg sodium, 1 g fiber*

Diet Exchanges: *0 milk, 0 vegetable, ½ fruit, 0 bread, ½ meat, 2 fat*

½ Carb Choice

100 Calories

Easiest Fruit Salad

—Brenda Michalak, Round Lake Beach, Illinois

*"Rather than reaching for a chocolate bar, cake, or cookies,
I make this sweet treat. It satisfies my craving for sweets
and it's a great snack between meals."*

Prep time: 10 minutes
Chill time: 1 hour

4 cups mixed fruit (strawberries,
  pineapple, kiwifruit, honeydew melon,
  seedless grapes, oranges, cantaloupe,
  mango, or blueberries), diced
1 tablespoon honey
¼ cup cranberry juice cocktail blend
⅛ teaspoon lemon or lime zest

In a large bowl, combine the fruit with the honey, juice, and zest. Chill, covered, for 1 hour.

Makes 4 servings

Per serving: *100 calories, 1 g protein, 26 g carbohydrate, 0 g fat, 0 mg cholesterol, 10 mg sodium, 0 g fiber*

Diet Exchanges: *0 milk, 0 vegetable, 1½ fruit, 0 bread, 0 meat, 0 fat*

2 Carb Choices

SHOPPING SAVVY
Melissa's Crazy Mixed-up Fruit

What do you get when you cross a plum (that's been crossed with an apricot) with a nectarine? A Nectacotum Pluot: A fruit that tastes like a plum, is shaped like a nectarine, and is haunted by an apricot. What do you get when you remove the reddish blush from a nectarine? A Mango Nectarine, tasting like mango with a nectarine's firmer texture. Confused? You won't be after sampling these fabulous fruits. Mango Nectarines and Nectacotum Pluots are only around from June to August, so bug your produce person and keep your eyes peeled. Distributed by Melissa's to produce sections nationwide. To locate a store near you, go to www.melissas.com.

Vegetable Soup

—Kathleen Johnson, Surrey, British Columbia, Canada

"This soup makes a very low-calorie but filling meal. It also has good protein and fat from the beans and a lot of healthy veggies."

Prep time: 15 minutes
Cook time: 20 minutes

1 onion, chopped

4 cloves garlic, finely chopped

4 large carrots, chopped

4 small Idaho potatoes, chopped

1 zucchini, sliced (optional)

1 can (28 ounces) diced tomatoes

1 can (15 ounces) mixed beans, rinsed and drained

1 package chili seasoning (mild or spicy)

Salt

Ground black pepper

In a large saucepot over medium heat, combine the onion, garlic, carrots, potatoes, and zucchini, if using. Pour in enough water to just cover the vegetables. Cook until the potatoes are soft, about 10 minutes.

Add the tomatoes, beans, and seasoning. Reduce the heat to low and simmer for 10 minutes. Season with salt and pepper to taste.

Makes 6 servings

Per serving: *152 calories, 8 g protein, 32 g carbohydrate, .5 g fat, 0 mg cholesterol, 362 mg sodium, 8 g fiber*

Diet Exchanges: *0 milk, 2 vegetable, 0 fruit, 1½ bread, 0 meat, 0 fat*

2 Carb Choices

It Worked for Me!

Danny Schwartz

VITAL STATS

Weight lost: 35 pounds

Time to goal: 8 months

Greatest challenge: Learning to eat in moderation

Danny Schwartz had been carrying some excess weight around for a while. He had a "gym habit," but his usual workouts just weren't doing the trick. Hiring a personal trainer provided the jumpstart he needed. This family-practice physician also improved his eating habits. Now, Danny finds that practicing what he preaches allows him to be an inspiration to his overweight patients.

"I knew my extra pounds were a problem. Both of my grandfathers died of heart attacks, and the real increase in obesity among my patients definitely got my attention. Many suffer from diabetes and other serious weight-related conditions. And, as a 'fat physician,' I found it hard to advise them to lose their own weight. Also, reading *Body for Life* by Bill Phillips was a real eye-opener.

"I started by hiring a personal trainer, who taught me serious weight lifting and changed my cardio workout a little bit. Basically my time at the gym became more intense and more effective.

"Then I addressed food and my relationship to it. The biggest thing I learned was portion control. I am an emotional eater and find it very hard to eat in moderation. I now eat small amounts, five or six times a day, and I see food as fuel. My serving sizes are never bigger than my fist. I've come to realize that the normal way most people eat—three overwhelming meals a day—does not work for me. And I'm sorry to say that I really didn't learn much about nutrition in medical school. I eat more fruits, vegetables, and nuts, and I only rarely indulge in less-healthy choices such as cheeseburgers, pizza, or steak.

"I was single when I finally got fed up with my weight, and it has been 4 years since I lost it. I like to joke that my wife wouldn't have gone out with me if I hadn't lost those pounds, but the fact is that losing weight did help me socially, as well as physically. And I feel much more comfortable coaching patients to lose weight; there are a number of great success stories in my practice now."

Cheesy Wild Rice and Spinach Soup

—Christa Coffen, Ontario, Canada

280 Calories

"Soups and stews are great for a low-fat lifestyle. They are filling, inherently healthy, and very easy to make low fat. Most soups can be made without 'sautéing' the vegetables in oil."

Prep time: 15 minutes
Cook time: 1 hour 10 minutes

   4 cups reduced-sodium chicken broth
   1 cup wild rice
   3 cups spinach, finely chopped
   ¼ cup flour
   4 cups low-fat milk
   ¾ teaspoon onion powder
   ½ teaspoon ground nutmeg
1½ cups shredded low-fat Swiss cheese
   2 tablespoons dry sherry
      Grated nutmeg (optional)

In a medium saucepan over medium-high heat, heat the broth and wild rice. Reduce the heat and let the rice cook for 60 to 70 minutes, or until it's tender. Do not drain. Stir in the spinach.

In a small bowl, mix together the flour and milk until smooth. Stir the flour mixture into the rice and spinach mixture. Add the onion powder and nutmeg. Cook over medium heat, stirring constantly, for about 10 minutes, or until the mixture thickens and begins to boil. Remove from the heat. Add the cheese and sherry and stir until the cheese is melted. Sprinkle with grated nutmeg, if using.

Makes 6 servings

Per serving: *280 calories, 21 g protein, 36 g carbohydrate, 6 g fat, 22 mg cholesterol, 229 mg sodium, 2 g fiber*

Diet Exchanges: *½ milk, 0 vegetable, 0 fruit, 2 bread, 1½ meat, 1 fat*

2½ Carb Choices

Butternut Bowl o' Soup

—Vikki Baird, Atlanta, Georgia

*"If you're lucky enough to have leftovers of this flavor-bursting soup,
it is actually better the next day!"*

116 Calories

Prep time: 15 minutes
Bake time: 60 minutes
Cook time: 5 minutes

1 butternut squash (about 2 pounds),
   halved and seeded
1 Vidalia onion, quartered
1 sweet potato, peeled and quartered
   Dash hot sauce
½ teaspoon curry
¼ teaspoon nutmeg
2 cups reduced-sodium chicken broth
   Salt
   Ground black pepper
½ cup fat-free half-and-half

Preheat the oven to 300°F. Coat a 13" × 9" baking dish with nonstick cooking spray. Place the squash cut-side down on the baking dish, and arrange the onion and potato sections around it. Bake for 60 minutes, or until the vegetables are tender. When the squash is cool enough to handle, remove the skin.

In a food processor, blend together the squash, onion, potato, hot sauce, curry, and nutmeg. Add the chicken broth as needed to thin the mixture.

Transfer the squash mixture to a large saucepot over medium heat, and stir in the remaining chicken broth. Cook for 5 minutes, or until warm. Season to taste with salt and pepper. Stir in the half-and-half just before serving.

Makes 6 servings

Per serving: *116 calories, 4 g protein, 26 g carbohydrate, 1 g fat, 0 mg cholesterol, 54 mg sodium, 4 g fiber*

Diet Exchanges: *0 milk, 2½ vegetable, 0 fruit, ½ bread, 0 meat, 0 fat*

1½ Carb Choices

Front, *Butternut Bowl o' Soup (opposite page)*
and Back, *Pepper Puree (page 70)*

138 Calories

Pepper Puree
—Marni Parker, Shelton, Washington

*"It's recipes like these that make dieting worthwhile.
Absolutely delicious!"*

**Prep time: 10 minutes
Cook time: 40 minutes**

1 tablespoon olive oil

1 large onion, finely chopped

1 clove garlic, finely chopped

3 roasted red bell peppers, chopped

4 cups reduced-sodium chicken broth

1 can (8 ounces) tomato sauce

  Salt

  Ground black pepper

  Juice of 1 lime

4 tablespoons low-fat or fat-fat sour cream
  (optional)

  Zest of 1 lime (optional)

Heat the oil in a large skillet over medium-high heat. Add the onion and garlic and cook for 2 minutes, or until the onion is slightly soft. Add the peppers and cook for another 2 minutes, or until the onion is translucent. Add 1 cup of the broth and cook for another 15 minutes.

Put the mixture in a blender and blend until smooth, adding another cup of broth as needed, and blending for about 1 second. Pour the mixture into a large saucepot. Add the remaining broth and the tomato sauce. Simmer for 20 minutes over low heat to let the flavors combine. Season with salt and pepper to taste.

Just before serving, stir in the lime juice. Top each serving with 1 tablespoon of sour cream and the lime zest for garnish, if using.

Makes 4 servings

Per serving: *138 calories, 7 g protein, 20 g carbohydrate, 5 g fat, 0 mg cholesterol, 371 mg sodium, 4 g fiber*

Diet Exchanges: *0 milk, 4 vegetable, 0 fruit, 0 bread, ½ meat, 1 fat*

1 Carb Choice

Kitchen Tip

To roast your own peppers, spread them on a baking sheet covered with aluminum foil and roast them under a broiler, positioning the baking sheet so it is about 3" below the heat source. Turn the peppers often, until the skin is charred black all over and is bubbling loose from the flesh.

When the peppers are cool enough to handle, pull out the stem and the core with its seeds. Peel off the skin with your fingers or the edge of a knife.

Italian Wedding Soup

240 Calories

—Julie McKenzie, Aliquippa, Pennsylvania

"This is a hearty, filling soup without a high fat content. A spin on a traditional Italian recipe."

Prep time: 10 minutes
Cook time: 15 minutes

- 4 large (48 ounce) cans reduced-sodium chicken broth
- 1 large boneless, skinless chicken breast half, chopped into ½" pieces
- ½ small onion, chopped (optional)
- ½ pound 90% lean ground beef
- ½ cup seasoned bread crumbs
- 1 teaspoon garlic powder
- 1 tablespoon grated Parmesan cheese
- 1 egg
- ½ package (10 ounces) frozen chopped spinach
- ½ cup orzo

In a large saucepan over high heat, bring the broth to a simmer. Add the chicken and onion and cook for 2 minutes, or until the chicken is cooked through.

In a large mixing bowl, combine the beef, bread crumbs, garlic powder, cheese, and egg. Roll the mixture into teaspoon-size balls, and drop them into the broth. Add the spinach. Let the soup cook for an additional 5 minutes, or until the meatballs are cooked. Remove from the heat.

Cook the orzo according to the package directions. Add it to the soup just before serving.

Makes 6 servings

Per serving: *240 calories, 22 g protein, 22 g carbohydrate, 7 g fat, 72 mg cholesterol, 329 mg sodium, 1 g fiber*

Diet Exchanges: *0 milk, 0 vegetable, 0 fruit, 1½ bread, 2½ meat, 1 fat*

1½ Carb Choices

Kitchen Tip

In Italian, orzo means "barley," but it's actually a tiny, rice-shaped pasta, slightly smaller than a pine nut. Orzo is ideal for soups and makes a wonderful rice substitute. In this recipe, you may also want to try other small pastinas.

Immunity-Boosting Turkey Soup

—Mary Tyrrell, Wyckoff, New Jersey

130 Calories

"Soup is always a good food for a weight-loss program because it fills you up without adding a lot of calories. I will have a cup of this soup half an hour before a meal to curb my appetite. It has the added benefits of being high in fiber and containing immunity-boosting ginger and garlic."

Prep time: 20 minutes
Cook time: 30 minutes

- 8 cups reduced-sodium turkey or chicken broth
- 2 carrots, chopped
- 2 ribs celery, chopped
- 1 onion, chopped
- 2 parsnips, chopped
- 1 tablespoon freshly grated ginger
- 2 cloves garlic, minced
- 3 tomatoes, chopped
- 1 cup cubed cooked turkey
  Salt
  Ground black pepper

Heat the broth in a large saucepan over medium heat. Add the carrots, celery, onion, parsnips, ginger, and garlic. Cook for 25 minutes, or until the vegetables are tender. Add the tomatoes and turkey. Cook for 5 minutes. Season with salt and pepper to taste.

Makes 6 servings

Per serving: *130 calories, 13 g protein, 16 g carbohydrate, 1.5 g fat, 20 mg cholesterol, 790 mg sodium, 4 g fiber*

Diet Exchanges: *0 milk, 1½ vegetable, 0 fruit, ½ bread, 1½ meat, 0 fat*

1 Carb Choice

SHOPPING SAVVY

Broth in a Box

Rich, hearty broth that's light on sodium is an essential ingredient in the calorie-conscious kitchen. Swanson fills the bill with a trio of organic broths. Toss that can opener back in the drawer—these come in easy-to-open, 32-ounce aseptic cartons. Organic Chicken Broth is from free-range chickens and is 99 percent fat free; Organic Beef Broth is from hormone- and antibiotic-free cattle and is 99 percent fat free; Organic Vegetable Broth is totally vegetarian and completely fat-free. All are lower in sodium than other broths on the market. All of them are handy for soups, simmering grains, saucing pasta, or to replace some oil with when sautéing. After opening, you can reseal the cartons and refrigerate for up to 2 weeks. Available nationwide.

Turkey Dumpling Delight

—Tyler McKinney, San Luis Obispo, California

431 Calories

Prep time: 15 minutes
Cook time: 35 minutes + 45 minutes to cook turkey

5 cups water
5 cups chicken broth
1 skinless turkey breast (4 to 5 pounds)
3 tablespoons + 1½ cups flour
1 cup milk
1 small rutabaga, chopped
1 rib celery, sliced
3 carrots, sliced
½ teaspoon ground black pepper
2 tablespoons parsley
1 tablespoon baking powder
¼ teaspoon salt
4 tablespoons trans-free margarine

Heat the water and the broth in a large stock pot over medium-high heat. When the broth begins to simmer, add the turkey breast, cover, and reduce the heat to low. Simmer for 45 to 50 minutes, or until the turkey breast is cooked through. Remove the turkey from the broth and set it aside to cool.

In a small bowl, combine 3 tablespoons of the flour with ½ cup of the milk. Pour the mixture into the broth. Cook, whisking constantly, for 2 minutes, or until the flour mixture dissolves. Add the rutabaga, celery, carrots, and pepper. Cook for 20 minutes, or until the vegetables are tender.

Remove the turkey from the bone. Chop it into small pieces and add 4 cups of chopped turkey to the soup. (Reserve the rest for another use.) Cook for 3 minutes, or until the turkey is heated through.

In a medium bowl, mix together the remaining 1½ cups of flour, parsley, baking powder, and salt just until combined. Add the remaining ½ cup of milk and the margarine. Mix until just blended.

Drop ¼-cup mounds of the dumpling mixture into the broth. Cover, cook for 6 minutes, then uncover and cook for another 6 minutes, or until the dumplings are dry in the center.

Makes 6 servings

Per serving: *431 calories, 44 g protein, 37 g carbohydrate, 10 g fat, 102 mg cholesterol, 1324 mg sodium, 3 g fiber*

Diet Exchanges: *0 milk, 1½ vegetable, 0 fruit, 2 bread, 5 meat, 1½ fat*

2½ Carb Choices

267 Calories

Turkey Chili

—Phyllis LaCroix, West Union, Illinois

"This recipe makes 8 servings, so I divide up leftovers into 1-cup servings and freeze them for later. It's a filling and satisfying quick fix for lunch."

Prep time: 10 minutes
Cook time: 20 minutes

2　tablespoons olive oil

1　pound lean ground turkey breast

1　package (1 ounce) reduced-sodium taco seasoning

1　cup corn

1　can (15 ounces) black beans, rinsed and drained

1　can (15 ounces) northern beans, rinsed and drained

1　can (15 ounces) pinto beans, rinsed and drained

1　can (16 ounces) reduced-sodium chicken broth

2　cans (14½ ounces each) tomatoes with chiles, with juice

　　Hot sauce (optional)

Spray a 6- to 8-quart pot with nonstick spray. Warm the oil in the pot over medium-high heat. When the oil's hot, add the turkey and cook for 5 minutes, or until it's no longer pink. Add the taco seasoning and stir until the meat is well coated with the seasoning. Add the corn, beans, broth, and tomatoes. Bring to a boil. Reduce the heat to medium-low and simmer, uncovered, for 20 minutes. Season to taste with hot sauce, if using.

Makes 8 servings

Per serving: *267 calories, 19 g protein, 29 g carbohydrate, 9 g fat, 45 mg cholesterol, 1127 mg sodium, 9 g fiber*

Diet Exchanges: *0 milk, 1 vegetable, 0 fruit, 1½ bread, 2 meat, 1 fat*

2 Carb Choices

Spicy Chicken Tortilla Soup

—Anita Lewis, Montgomery, Alabama

120 Calories

"My husband and I really enjoy this spicy and delicious soup. It's nice to make something homemade that's healthy, so I don't feel like I'm cheating on my diet."

Prep time: 15 minutes
Cook time: 22 minutes

3 cups reduced-sodium chicken broth

2 boneless, skinless chicken breast halves

1 small tomato, chopped

½ large white onion, chopped

½ jalapeño chile pepper, seeded and chopped (wear plastic gloves when handling)

2 tablespoons jarred, pickled jalapeño chile peppers, chopped

2 tablespoons chopped cilantro

1 can (14½ ounces) diced tomatoes

1 teaspoon minced onion

2 teaspoons Southwest seasoning

1 can (15 ounces) black beans, drained and rinsed

1 package (8 ounces) shredded Monterey Jack cheese (optional)

3 low-carb tortillas, 8" each, torn into strips and baked (optional; see Kitchen Tip)

In a large saucepot over high heat, add the broth and chicken. Cook for 12 minutes, or until the chicken is cooked through. Transfer the chicken to a cutting board. When it's cool enough to handle, chop the chicken into small pieces, and set aside.

In a food processor, blend together the tomato, onion, jalapeños, and cilantro. Add to the broth. Add the diced tomatoes, onion, seasoning, black beans, and chicken. Cook for 5 to 10 more minutes, stirring occasionally. Serve with the cheese and tortilla strips, if using.

Makes 6 servings

Per serving: *120 calories, 11 g protein, 16 g carbohydrate, 2 g fat, 11 mg cholesterol, 476 mg sodium, 4 g fiber*

Diet Exchanges: *0 milk, 1 vegetable, 0 fruit, ½ bread, 1 meat, 0 fat*

1 Carb Choice

┌─ *Kitchen Tip* ─────────────
Preheat your oven to 350°F and coat a baking sheet with nonstick spray. Bake the tortilla strips for about 10 minutes, or until they're lightly browned and crispy.
└──────────────────────────

Slow Cooker Black Bean Chili

—Kim Kindrew, Hampton, Virginia

139 Calories

"Reducing meat in my diet has not only helped me to lose weight, but has lowered my cholesterol, as well. This recipe is hearty and filling, high in fiber, yet low in calories and fat. Plus, it cooks while I'm at work, so it's ready when I get home!"

Prep time: 10 minutes
Cook time: 3–4 hours

2 cans (14½ ounces each) black beans, drained

2 cans (14½ ounces each) diced tomatoes with chiles, drained

1 cup corn

1 bunch scallions, finely chopped

2 cloves garlic, finely chopped

1 tablespoon chili powder

1 teaspoon cumin

1 teaspoon cocoa powder

½ teaspoon salt

¼ teaspoon pepper

½ bunch cilantro, minced (optional)

1 container (8 ounces) low-fat sour cream (optional)

Baked tortilla chips (optional)

In a 6-quart slow cooker, combine the beans, tomatoes, corn, scallions, garlic, chili powder, cumin, cocoa powder, salt, and pepper. Cook for 3 to 4 hours on high.

Garnish each serving with cilantro and sour cream. Serve with tortilla chips, if using.

Makes 6 servings

Per serving: *139 calories, 8 g protein, 24 g carbohydrate, 1 g fat, 0 mg cholesterol, 717 mg sodium, 8 g fiber*

Diet Exchanges: *0 milk, 1½ vegetable, 0 fruit, 1 bread, ½ meat, 0 fat*

1½ Carb Choices

197 Calories

Spicy Cabbage Soup
—Sandra Riccardi, Ferndale, Michigan

Prep time: 8 minutes
Cook time: 35 minutes

1 pound 94% fat-free ground turkey breast

1 onion, chopped

2 cloves garlic, finely chopped

2 ribs celery, sliced

½ head cabbage, chopped

1 can (10 ounces) diced tomatoes with chile peppers

4 cups reduced-sodium chicken broth

1 cup reduced-sodium tomato vegetable juice

½ teaspoon chili powder

Juice of 1 lemon

1 cup frozen green beans

Salt

Ground black pepper

Hot sauce

Coat a large saucepan with nonstick cooking spray and place it over medium-high heat. Add the turkey and cook for 5 minutes, or until no longer pink. Remove the turkey, and set it aside.

Add the onion, garlic, celery, and cabbage to the saucepan. Cook for 10 minutes, or until the vegetables are tender. Add the tomatoes, broth, juice, chili powder, and lemon juice. Let simmer for 10 minutes. Add the green beans and simmer for 10 minutes more, or until the green beans are tender. Season with the salt, pepper, and hot sauce to taste.

Makes 6 servings

Per serving: *197 calories, 19 g protein, 16 g carbohydrate, 7 g fat, 60 mg cholesterol, 310 mg sodium, 4 g fiber*

Diet Exchanges: *0 milk, 2½ vegetable, 0 fruit, 0 bread, 2½ meat, ½ fat*

1 Carb Choice

Chunky Chicken Stew

—Jennifer Maslowski, New York, New York

"This recipe is great if you love spicy soups and stews!"

Prep time: 15 minutes
Cook time: 1 hour 30 minutes

1 tablespoon olive oil

1 medium yellow or white onion, coarsely chopped

½ teaspoon salt

2 cloves garlic, minced

1 pound chicken breast, cut into 1½" cubes

3 russet potatoes, peeled and cut into large cubes

1 pound carrots, cleaned and cut into 1" pieces

3 cans (15 ounces each) low-sodium vegetable broth

1 can (14½ ounces) whole green beans, with liquid

½ cup ketchup

1 box (10 ounces) frozen peas

3 tablespoons Worcestershire sauce

1 teaspoon hot paprika

½ teaspoon black pepper

½ teaspoon red pepper flakes

In an 8-quart stockpot or Dutch oven, heat the oil over medium heat.

Add the onion and salt and cook for 5 minutes, or until the onion is translucent.

Add the garlic, and cook for 4 minutes, or until golden. Add the chicken and cook for 10 minutes, or until no longer pink.

Add the potatoes, carrots, broth, green beans, and ketchup. Cook until the stew boils, stirring occasionally.

Reduce the heat to low and add the peas, Worcestershire sauce, paprika, black pepper, and red pepper. Cook for 1 hour, or until the potatoes and carrots are tender.

Makes 8 servings

Per serving: *260 calories, 19 g protein, 34 g carbohydrate, 6 g fat, 33 mg cholesterol, 945 mg sodium, 7 g fiber*

Diet Exchanges: *0 milk, 3½ vegetable, 0 fruit, 1 bread, 2 meat, 1 fat*

2 Carb Choices

299 Calories

Posole

—D. Summers, Richardson, Texas

"If you like heat, add more chili powder, but if you're more mild, reduce the chili powder to 1 tablespoon."

Prep time: 10 minutes
Cook time: 40 minutes

- 1 tablespoon olive oil
- 1 pound 95% lean ground beef
- ½ pound reduced-fat pork sausage, crumbled
- 1 can (28 ounces) hominy
- 1 can (15 ounces) tomato sauce
- 1 can (28 ounces) diced tomatoes
- 2 tablespoons chili powder
- 1 teaspoon cumin
- 1 canned chipotle pepper, finely chopped
- 1 teaspoon ground red pepper (optional)

Heat the oil in a 6- to 8-quart pot or Dutch oven over medium-high heat. Add the beef and sausage. Cook for about 12 minutes, or until cooked through. Drain off all the fat.

Add the hominy, tomato sauce, tomatoes, chili powder, cumin, pepper, and red pepper, and cook for 30 minutes. If the mixture begins to look too thick, add a small amount of water.

Makes 6 servings (11 cups)

Per serving: *299 calories, 22 g protein, 36 g carbohydrate, 8 g fat, 48 mg cholesterol, 1119 mg sodium, 7 g fiber*

Diet Exchanges: *0 milk, 2½ vegetable, 0 fruit, 1½ bread, 2½ meat, 1 fat*

2½ Carb Choices

Irish Pork Stew with Irish Stout and Caraway Seeds

362 Calories

—Elizabeth Martlock, Jim Thorpe, Pennsylvania

Prep time: 15 minutes
Cook time: 1 hour

⅓ cup flour

1½ teaspoons salt

¼ teaspoon pepper

2 pounds boneless pork shoulder, cut into 1½" cubes and carefully trimmed of all visible excess fat

1 teaspoon vegetable oil

4 large onions, chopped

1 clove garlic, finely chopped

½ bunch parsley, finely chopped

1 teaspoon caraway seeds

1 bay leaf

1⅓ cups reduced-sodium chicken broth

1 bottle (12 ounces) Irish stout, such as Guinness

2 tablespoons red wine vinegar

1 tablespoon brown sugar, packed

Salt

Ground black pepper

In a large, resealable plastic bag, combine the flour, salt, and pepper. Add the pork and shake to coat the pieces.

Heat the oil in a large Dutch oven over medium-high heat. Add the pork and cook for 5 minutes, or until the pork has browned on all sides. Reduce the heat to medium. Add the onions and garlic and cook for 4 minutes, or until the onions are soft. Add the parsley, caraway seeds, bay leaf, broth, beer, vinegar, and sugar. Add salt and pepper to taste. Reduce the heat to low-medium, and, stirring frequently, cook for 1 to 1½ hours, or until the pork becomes very tender.

Makes 6 servings

Per serving: *362 calories, 34 g protein, 25 g carbohydrate, 12 g fat, 101 mg cholesterol, 724 mg sodium, 4 g fiber*

Diet Exchanges: *0 milk, 2½ vegetable, 0 fruit, 1 bread, 4½ meat, 0 fat*

2 Carb Choices

Sandwiches, Snacks, and Sides

SANDWICHES

SNACKS

SIDES

Kickin' Sloppy Joes

462 Calories

—Amy Lyn Miller, Bealeton, Virginia

*"This is my favorite homemade dish. It's healthy and delicious!
I hope others will enjoy it as much as my family and I have."*

**Prep time: 5 minutes
Cook time: 20 minutes**

1½ pounds lean ground turkey
¼ pound mushrooms, sliced
½ teaspoon garlic powder
1 cup ketchup
¼ cup apple cider vinegar
2 tablespoons yellow mustard
¼ cup Worcestershire sauce
    Ground red pepper
8 slices low-carb whole wheat bread,
    or 4 rolls

Coat a large skillet with cooking spray and place it over medium heat. Add the turkey and mushrooms, and cook for 2 to 3 minutes, or until browned. Add the garlic powder. Reduce the heat to low and cook for 3 minutes. Stir in the ketchup. Add the vinegar, mustard, and Worcestershire sauce. Continue cooking over low heat for 5 to 10 minutes, stirring occasionally. Add the ground red pepper to taste, if using. Remove from the heat. Spoon the mixture over 4 of the slices of bread or the bottom halves of the rolls, and top with the remaining slices of bread or the tops of the rolls.

Makes 4 servings

Per serving: *462 calories, 40 g protein, 39 g carbohydrate, 18 g fat, 135 mg cholesterol, 1354 mg sodium, 7 g fiber*

Diet Exchanges: *0 milk, 1 vegetable, 0 fruit, 2 bread, 5 meat, 2 fat*

2½ Carb Choices

Turkey Mozzarella Bake

—Allison Perritt, Primm Springs, Tennessee

239 Calories

"This easy dish provides all the delicious and filling flavors of my favorite sandwich, without all the bread."

Prep time: 5 minutes
Cook time: 7 minutes

8 slices turkey or ham

2 tomatoes, cut into 8 slices

8 teaspoons fat-free or low-fat mayo

8 slices mozzarella cheese

Preheat the oven to 350°F.

Place a slice of the turkey on each tomato slice. Spread 1 teaspoon of mayonnaise onto each slice of turkey. Top the mayonnaise with a slice of mozzarella cheese.

Place the tomatoes on a baking sheet and bake in the oven for about 7 minutes, or until the cheese has melted and is toasty brown.

Makes 4 servings

Per serving: *239 calories, 20 g protein, 8 g carbohydrate, 14 g fat, 64 mg cholesterol, 864 mg sodium, 1 g fiber*

Diet Exchanges: *0 milk, 1 vegetable, 0 fruit, 0 bread, 3 meat, 2 fat*

½ **Carb Choice**

Gianna's Savory Chicken Sandwiches

—Giovanna Kranenberg, Cambridge, Minnesota

212 Calories

"This sandwich tastes great on sourdough, wheat, or regular bread. It tastes best if you let it marinate for a while in the fridge—that is, if you can wait!"

Prep time: 10 minutes

1 large can (10 ounces) white chicken
6 baby carrots, diced
1 stalk celery, diced
1 clove garlic, minced
⅓ cup Italian mild Giardiniera, drained and chopped
2 tablespoons diced white onion
¼ cup low-fat or fat-free mayonnaise
Salt
Ground black pepper
12 slices of your favorite bread
6 lettuce leaves

Drain the chicken and place it in a large bowl. Add the carrots, celery, garlic, Giardiniera, onion, and mayonnaise. Combine well. Salt and pepper to taste.

Cover 1 slice of bread with ½ cup of the chicken salad. Add one lettuce leaf and another slice of bread.

Makes 6 servings

Per serving: *212 calories, 15 g protein, 31 g carbohydrate, 5 g fat, 17 mg cholesterol, 641 mg sodium, 5 g fiber*

Diet Exchanges: *0 milk, ½ vegetable, 0 fruit, 2 bread, 1½ meat, ½ fat*

2 Carb Choices

Tomato and Basil Flatbread Pizza

—Ann Muth, Louisville, Kentucky

307 Calories

"This pizza is super-quick and delicious."

Prep time: 5 minutes
Cook time: 7 minutes

2 tablespoons pesto sauce
2 flatbreads, each about 7" across
1 tomato, thinly sliced
1 tablespoon basil
¼ cup shredded mozzarella cheese

Preheat the oven to 425°F.

Spread the pesto on the bread. Add a layer of tomato and a layer of basil. Sprinkle the cheese over the top. Bake for 7 minutes, or until the cheese is golden and melted.

Makes 2 servings

Per serving: *307 calories, 12 g protein, 40 g carbohydrate, 11 g fat, 16 mg cholesterol, 531 mg sodium, 3 g fiber*

Diet Exchanges: *0 milk, 1 vegetable, 0 fruit, 2½ bread, 1 meat, 2 fat*

3 Carb Choices

Slimmed-Down Veggie Quesadillas

—Sue Cooper, San Jose, California

377 Calories

"I used to eat a full-fat version of quesadillas: regular tortillas, regular cheese and sour cream, fried in oil, and so on. This slimmed-down version is both lower in fat and more filling because of the added vegetables."

Prep time: 10 minutes
Cook time: 7 minutes

1 large carrot, peeled and thinly sliced

¼ pound mushrooms, thinly sliced

1 large zucchini, halved and thinly sliced

1 teaspoon garlic powder

8 plain or flavored 99% fat-free tortillas (8" in diameter)

1 package (4 ounces) reduced-fat shredded Mexican cheese

1 cup salsa

1 cup fat-free sour cream

Preheat the oven to 400°F. Coat a baking sheet with cooking spray. Coat a skillet with cooking spray and place it over medium heat. Add the carrot and cook for 1 minute. Add the mushrooms and zucchini, and cook for 4 minutes, or until the carrots are tender. Toss with the garlic powder.

Place 4 tortillas on the baking sheet and sprinkle them with half the cheese. Add a layer of the vegetables and top with the remaining cheese. Gently press the remaining tortillas on top.

Bake for 6 to 8 minutes, or until the tortillas look crisp and the cheese is melted.

Cut the quesadillas into wedges. Serve with the salsa and sour cream.

Makes 4 servings

Per serving: *377 calories, 20 g protein, 67 g carbohydrate, 4 g fat, 9 mg cholesterol, 1096 mg sodium, 5 g fiber*

Diet Exchanges: *0 milk, 2 vegetable, 0 fruit, 4 bread, 1 meat, ½ fat*

4½ Carb Choices

Burger with Mushrooms

187 Calories

—D. Summers, Richardson, Texas

"With this burger alongside a couple of veggies, I am completely satisfied."

Prep time: 25 minutes
Chill time: 20 minutes
Cook time: 30 minutes

½ **pound mushrooms, cleaned**
½ **onion**
3 **teaspoons olive oil**
1 **clove garlic, finely chopped**
1 **pound 97% lean ground beef**
1 **tablespoon Worcestershire sauce**
1 **teaspoon Dijon mustard**
  Salt
  Ground black pepper

Finely chop 8 mushrooms, and slice the remaining mushrooms. Finely chop half of the onion, and slice the remaining onion. Set the sliced vegetables aside.

Heat 1 teaspoon of oil in a nonstick skillet over medium heat. Add the chopped onion and cook for about 6 minutes, or until it's soft. Add the garlic and continue cooking for another minute.

Add 1 teaspoon of the remaining oil. Add the chopped mushrooms and cook for about 5 minutes. Allow the veggies to cool for 5 minutes.

In a large mixing bowl, combine the onion and mushroom mixture, ground beef, Worcestershire sauce, and mustard. Add salt and pepper to taste. Form into 4 patties. Chill in the refrigerator for about 20 minutes to set.

In the same skillet, heat the remaining 1 teaspoon of oil. Add the sliced mushrooms and sliced onions, and cook until tender, about 5 minutes. Move the mushroom mixture from the pan to a plate. Cover with foil to keep warm.

In the same pan, cook the meat patties for 5 to 7 minutes on each side, or until the internal temperature measures 160°F on an instant-read thermometer and the meat is no longer pink. Serve the patties topped with the mushroom mixture.

Makes 4 servings

Per serving: *187 calories, 24 g protein, 5 g carbohydrate, 8 g fat, 60 mg cholesterol, 143 mg sodium, 1 g fiber*

Diet Exchanges: *0 milk, 1 vegetable, 0 fruit, 0 bread, 3 meat, 1 fat*

½ **Carb Choice**

Hot Beef Pita Pocket

—Sandy Umber, Springdale, Arizona

*"This takes away my craving for those hot Italian beef sandwiches
I gobbled down as a teen. It satisfies and fills me up."*

265
Calories

Prep time: 10 minutes
Cook time: 15 minutes

1 pound lean roast beef, thinly sliced into
strips

1 onion, sliced

1 green bell pepper, sliced into rounds

1 red bell pepper, sliced into rounds

1 chile pepper, thinly sliced

Salt

Ground black pepper

2 whole wheat pitas

Coat a large nonstick saucepan with cooking spray.

Add the beef and cook for 4 to 6 minutes. Remove the beef and add the onion, and cook for 2 minutes. Add the peppers and cook for 5 minutes, or until the peppers are slightly softened. Return the beef to the pan and cook for 1 minute. Add salt and pepper to taste. Slice each pita in half, and stuff each half with the beef mixture.

Makes 4 servings

Per serving: *265 calories, 30 g protein, 26 g carbohydrate, 6 g fat, 66 mg cholesterol, 239 mg sodium, 4 g fiber*

Diet Exchanges: *0 milk, 1½ vegetable, 0 fruit, 1 bread, 4 meat, ½ fat*

2 Carb Choices

Fall Cream Cheese Dip

—Kim Hilbert, Freedom, Pennsylvania

"This delicious dip became a great incentive for me to eat more fresh fruit."

Prep time: 5 minutes

¼ **cup brown sugar**

1 **package (8 ounces) reduced-fat cream cheese**

Juice of 1 lemon or 4 tablespoons water

2 **medium apples, sliced**

In a medium bowl, combine the brown sugar and cream cheese, mixing with a fork until well combined. Add the lemon juice or water and stir until smooth. Serve with the apple slices.

Makes 4 servings

Per serving: *209 calories, 6 g protein, 25 g carbohydrate, 10 g fat, 32 mg cholesterol, 173 mg sodium, 3 g fiber*

Diet Exchanges: *0 milk, 0 vegetable, 1 fruit, ½ bread, 1 meat, 2 fat*

1½ Carb Choices

28 Calories

Artichoke Mélange

—Emily Ferrini, Mount Prospect, Illinois

Prep time: 15 minutes

- ¼ cup shredded Asiago cheese
- 2 tablespoons low-fat sour cream
- 2 tablespoons reduced-fat mayonnaise
- 1 jar (7½ ounces) marinated artichoke hearts, drained and diced
- ½ cup black olives, pitted and diced
- ½ cup diced plum tomatoes
- ½ teaspoon garlic salt
- ¼ teaspoon ground black pepper

In a medium bowl, combine the cheese, sour cream, and mayonnaise until smooth. Add the artichoke hearts, olives, tomatoes, garlic salt, and black pepper. Gently fold until the ingredients are well-coated with the cheese mixture. Cover and chill for at least 30 minutes, or up to 24 hours before serving. Serve with crackers or chips.

Makes 16 servings, 2 tablespoons each (2 cups)

Per serving: *28 calories, 1 g protein, 2 g carbohydrate, 2 g fat, 2 mg cholesterol, 129 mg sodium, 1 g fiber*

Diet Exchanges: *0 milk, 0 vegetable, 0 fruit, 0 bread, 0 meat, ½ fat*

0 Carb Choice

Cottage Cheese Dill Dip

—Angela King, Cincinnati, Ohio

"This dip makes a great snack—it helps me avoid reaching for high-fat and -calorie snacks and dips when I'm also making dinner."

20 Calories

Prep time: 5 minutes

- 1 cup fat-free cottage cheese
- ¼ teaspoon onion powder
- ½ teaspoon garlic salt
- 1 teaspoon chopped fresh dill weed, or ½ teaspoon dried dill weed

In a food processor, combine the cottage cheese, onion powder, garlic salt, and dill. Pulse until smooth, about 30 seconds.

Serve as dip for raw vegetables or fat-free tortilla chips.

Makes 8 servings, 2 tablespoons each (1 cup)

Per serving: *20 calories, 3 g protein, 2 g carbohydrate, 0 g fat, 1 mg cholesterol, 170 mg sodium, 0 g fiber*

Diet Exchanges: *0 milk, 0 vegetable, 0 fruit, 0 bread, ½ meat, 0 fat*

0 Carb Choice

17 Calories

Black Bean Salsa

—Jo Dufay, Ottawa, Ontario, Canada

"This super-easy salsa is fresh tasting, low in fat, high in fiber, and protein rich. It tastes like sun-ripened tomatoes, even in the winter."

Prep time: 12 minutes

1 can (15 ounces) black beans, drained

3 medium tomatoes, diced

2 tablespoons frozen orange juice concentrate

½ cup chopped cilantro

Salt

In a medium bowl, mix the beans, tomatoes, orange juice, and cilantro. Add salt to taste. Let the mixture stand for 30 minutes to allow the flavors to combine.

Makes 28 servings (3½ cups)

Per serving: *17 calories, 1 g protein, 3 g carbohydrate, 0 g fat, 0 mg cholesterol, 40 mg sodium, 1 g fiber*

Diet Exchanges: *0 milk, 0 vegetable, 0 fruit, 0 bread, 0 meat, 0 fat*

0 Carb Choice

It Worked for Me!

Barbara Orland

VITAL STATS

Weight lost: 20 pounds

Time to goal: About a year

Greatest challenge: Beating a nervous eating habit

Barbara Orland was never a "healthy eater." Even—or especially—when dieting, she would find herself falling off the good-intentions wagon and eating more junk food than usual. Beating her emotional binge eating habits and adding exercise has allowed Barbara to get rid of her spare pounds once and for all.

"My weight had always been a little bit of a problem. When I was a kid, I remember having to wear the 'Chubettes' brand clothes made just for overweight kids. After I had my own children, I added more weight. I started to worry that after menopause things would get even worse.

"I know that my problem is mostly emotional eating—I'll snack unconsciously when I'm nervous and just can't follow regimented eating plans. Learning to make smarter, healthier choices (instead of following a strict "diet") helped me to lose weight. For example, if I know I just want to eat for the sake of eating, I'll have a huge salad. This is low-cal and full of vitamins, and gives me something satisfying to chew on for a while.

"To get even more vegetables into my daily diet, I now roast things. I find that I can eat a mound of delicious roasted vegetables with no need to feel guilty for filling up. Of course, from time to time, my husband and I do like to enjoy cheese and crackers with our wine, but staying aware of the food choices I make most of the time gives me the leeway I need to indulge myself once in a while. I'll admit that I allow myself a sweet treat every single day—but it's low-fat frozen yogurt, and not a big scoop of regular ice cream. I have learned to discriminate that way, and it makes all the difference.

"Exercise is also a big help. I get moving for an hour every day, even if that means I have to do four little 15-minute sessions to get it all in. I'll walk for 15 minutes before the kids go to school, then 15 minutes before and after lunch, and another 15 when I get home. Every minute really does count!"

40 Calories

Guacamole Dip

—Kathleen Lyons, Fort Wayne, Indiana

"I use this dip instead of sour cream on Mexican food."

Prep time: 8 minutes

2 avocados
½ cup prepared salsa
1 clove garlic, minced
1 teaspoon lemon juice
¼ cup plain yogurt
  Salt

Remove the pit from the avocados, scrape out the pulp, and mash it in a mixing bowl. Add the salsa, garlic, lemon juice, and yogurt. Season with salt to taste. Mix well to combine. Stir before serving.

Makes 16 servings, 2 tablespoons each (2 cups)

Per serving: *40 calories, 1 g protein, 3 g carbohydrate, 3 g fat, 0 mg cholesterol, 33 mg sodium, 2 g fiber*

Diet Exchanges: *0 milk, 0 vegetable, 0 fruit, 0 bread, 0 meat, 1 fat*

0 Carb Choice

Kitchen Tip

To cut an avocado, use a chef's knife and cut it in half from top to bottom through the peel and around the pit. Twist the halves apart. Place the half containing the pit face up in your hand or on a cutting board (nest it in a towel if it falls to one side). Whack the pit with the blade of the knife. Twist the knife and lift out the pit.

5 Calories

Spicy Jalapeño Salsa

—Heather Arent-Zachary, Seattle, Washington

"This salsa is great with baked tortilla chips, on tacos, and as a sauce for fish or chicken."

Prep time: 10 minutes
Cook time: 5 minutes

1 cup water
2 jalapeño chile peppers
2 cloves garlic
¼ small onion, chopped
1 can (28 ounces) whole tomatoes, drained
2 small bunches cilantro, chopped
2 tablespoons fresh lime juice
Chili powder
Salt
Ground black pepper

Bring the water to a boil in a small pot, add the peppers, reduce the heat, and simmer for 5 minutes. Remove the peppers with a slotted spoon and reserve the water. Slice the stems off the peppers and discard. Place the peppers in a blender with the reserved cooking water, garlic, onion, tomatoes, and half the cilantro. Blend for about 20 seconds, or until well mixed. Stir in the lime juice and the remaining cilantro. Add chili powder, salt, and pepper to taste.

Makes 24 servings, 2 tablespoons each (3 cups)

Per serving: *5 calories, 0 g protein, 1 g carbohydrate, 0 g fat, 0 mg cholesterol, 16 mg sodium, 0 g fiber*

Diet Exchanges: *0 milk, 0 vegetable, 0 fruit, 0 bread, 0 meat, 0 fat*

0 Carb Choice

Kitchen Tip

If the jalapeño chile peppers you're using are particularly hot, you might want to minimize the heat in this dish by scraping out the seeds and veins that line the inside of the peppers' flesh after you cut off the stems. It's a good idea to wear plastic gloves when doing this.

Honey Barbecue Drummettes

—Mike Young, Cantonment, Florida

205 Calories

Prep time: 20 minutes
Marinate time: 2 hours
Cook time: 15 minutes

 2 **pounds chicken drummettes**
⅓ **cup honey**
⅓ **cup tomato sauce**
 1 **teaspoon grated ginger**
 1 **teaspoon soy sauce**
 1 **teaspoon Worcestershire sauce**

Pull the skin off the drummettes and discard it; place the drummettes in a large, resealable plastic bag.

In a mixing bowl, combine the honey, tomato sauce, ginger, soy sauce, and Worcestershire sauce. Pour over the drummettes. Refrigerate for 2 hours.

Preheat the oven to 350°F. Line a rimmed baking sheet with aluminum foil and coat it with cooking spray. Remove the drumettes from the marinade and arrange them on the baking sheet. Bake for 15 minutes.

Makes 4 servings

Per serving: *205 calories, 19 g protein, 24 g carbohydrate, 4 g fat, 71 mg cholesterol, 326 mg sodium, 0 g fiber*

Diet Exchanges: *0 milk, 0 vegetable, 0 fruit, 1½ bread, 2½ meat, 0 fat*

1½ Carb Choices

SHOPPING SAVVY
A Great Grater and a Terrific Turner

OXO Good Grips has a better idea when it comes to kitchen accessories. We loved these two new tools: The i-Series Container Grater and the Nylon Flexible Turner.

The grater makes fine shreds of Parmesan or citrus zest, and the blade works in both directions—up and down. A graduated container that snaps onto the back holds and measures whatever you're grating. The turner is kind to nonstick pans, easily pries up food that needs turning or lifting, and is heat-and dishwasher-safe. Available in bright colors with cool names: Blueberry, Raspberry, Pesto, Tomato, Pumpkin, and Black. Sold at housewares stores.

Oven Fries

—Ned Loughborough, San Antonio, Texas

150 Calories

"I love french fries, and these don't have all the fat that's normally involved, and they're just as flavorful. For a nice crunch, put the cooked fries under the broiler for a few seconds."

Prep time: 5 minutes
Cook time: 20 minutes

   2 large russet potatoes, sliced into ¼"-thick lengthwise strips
   1 egg white, lightly beaten
   ¼ teaspoon paprika
      Salt
      Ground black pepper

Preheat the oven to 400°F. Coat a baking sheet with cooking spray.

Brush the potatoes with the egg white. Sprinkle with the paprika. Bake for about 20 minutes, or until the fries are nicely browned. Season with salt and pepper to taste.

Makes 4 servings

Per serving: *150 calories, 5 g protein, 33 g carbohydrate, 0 g fat, 0 mg cholesterol, 23 mg sodium, 2 g fiber*

Diet Exchanges: *0 milk, 0 vegetable, 0 fruit, 2 bread, 0 meat, 0 fat*

2 Carb Choices

208 Calories Chickpea Delight

—Carmen Keithly, Austin, Texas

"I keep this salad in my fridge. When hunger strikes, I don't have to go for the simple carbs—I can enjoy a healthy meal. It will keep in the refrigerator in a well-sealed container for 2 or 3 days."

Prep time: 10 minutes

1 avocado, pitted and cubed

2 tomatoes, chopped

2 tablespoons fat-free sour cream

¼ teaspoon hot paprika

Juice of ½ of 1 lime

Salt

Freshly ground black pepper

8 cups romaine lettuce, chopped

1 can (15½ ounces) chickpeas, rinsed and drained

½ cup chopped cilantro

2 carrots, shredded

In a small bowl, mix together the avocado, tomatoes, sour cream, paprika, lime juice, and salt and pepper to taste.

In a large bowl, combine the romaine, chickpeas, cilantro, and carrots. Add the avocado mixture, and toss gently.

Makes 4 servings

Per serving: *208 calories, 8 g protein, 29 g carbohydrate, 8 g fat, 0 mg cholesterol, 309 mg sodium, 12 g fiber*

Diet Exchanges: *0 milk, 2 vegetable, ½ fruit, 1 bread, 0 meat, 1 fat*

2 Carb Choices

SHOPPING SAVVY
Thirsty?

Instead of reaching for a sugar-laden soda, quench your thirst with a crisp, clear, chilled bottle of Fruit$_2$0. Sweet and bursting with delicious fruit flavor, this spring water contains zero calories and no carbs because it's sweetened with Splenda. Fruit$_2$0 comes in an orchard of flavors including peach, orange, lemon, cherry, lime, raspberry, grape, and strawberry. Sold in most grocery and convenience stores.

Stir-Fried Broccoli

70 Calories

—Linda Chaput, Rutherglen, Ontario, Canada

"For a change of pace, try cauliflower instead of broccoli."

Prep time: 5 minutes
Cook time: 5 minutes

1 large head broccoli
1 tablespoon olive oil
1 tablespoon lemon juice
2 drops hot chili oil
   Ground black pepper

Cut the broccoli into florets. Peel the stalks, and cut them into 1" pieces.

Place a steamer basket in a large pot with 2" of water. Bring to a boil over high heat. Place the broccoli in the basket and steam for about 1 minute. Drain.

In a medium, nonstick skillet, heat the olive oil over medium-high heat. Add the broccoli and cook for 2 to 3 minutes, or until crisp-tender. Squeeze the lemon juice over the broccoli. Toss with the chili oil and add pepper to taste.

Makes 4 servings

Per serving: *70 calories, 3 g protein, 7 g carbohydrate, 4 g fat, 0 mg cholesterol, 35 mg sodium, 3 g fiber*

Diet Exchanges: *0 milk, 1½ vegetable, 0 fruit, 0 bread, 0 meat, 1 fat*

½ **Carb Choice**

Stir-Fried Kale with Almonds

126 Calories

—Teresa Mattson, Ormond Beach, Florida

"This tasty dish is easy, filling, healthy, and even vegan!"

Prep time: 10 minutes
Cook time: 7 minutes

  2 **tablespoons olive oil**
  1 **large clove garlic, finely chopped**
  1 **teaspoon grated ginger**
  ¼ **cup slivered almonds**
1½ **pounds kale, stems removed, chopped into 1" pieces**
  1 **tablespoon tamari**
  2 **tablespoons low-sodium vegetable broth**

In a large nonstick skillet, heat the oil over medium-high heat. Add the garlic and ginger and cook for 30 seconds.

Reduce the heat to medium. Add the almonds and cook for 1 minute. Add the kale, tamari, and broth. Cook for about 5 minutes, or until the kale is wilted but not soggy.

Makes 6 servings

Per serving: *126 calories, 5 g protein, 13 g carbohydrate, 8 g fat, 0 mg cholesterol, 212 mg sodium, 3 g fiber*

Diet Exchanges: *0 milk, 2½ vegetable, 0 fruit, 0 bread, 0 meat, 1 fat*

1 Carb Choice

Glazed Carrots with Pineapple

—Phyllis LaCroix, West Union, Illinois

56 Calories

"These delicious carrots really satisfy my sweet tooth."

Prep time: 5 minutes
Cook time: 15 minutes

  1 **pound carrots, peeled and sliced**
  ½ **cup water**
  ½ **cup crushed pineapple with juice**
  2 **teaspoons cornstarch**
  ½ **teaspoon salt**
  1 **teaspoon trans-free margarine**
  1 **tablespoon sugar substitute**

Put the carrots in a microwaveable bowl with 3 to 4 tablespoons of water, cover with plastic wrap, and microwave on high for 3 to 4 minutes, or until tender.

In a large saucepot over medium-high heat, combine the water, pineapple, cornstarch, and salt. Cook over medium-high heat, stirring constantly, until the mixture comes to a boil. Boil for 1 minute. Add the margarine, sugar substitute, and carrots. Cook for about 5 minutes, or until the carrots are glazed.

Makes 6 servings

Per serving: *56 calories, 1 g protein, 12 g carbohydrate, 1 g fat, 0 mg cholesterol, 241 mg sodium, 2 g fiber*

Diet Exchanges: *0 milk, 1 vegetable, ½ fruit, 0 bread, 0 meat, 0 fat*

1 Carb Choice

Sautéed Yellow Squash, Zucchini, and Onions

—Elizabeth Martlock, Jim Thorpe, Pennsylvania

Prep time: 5 minutes
Cook time: 13 minutes

2 tablespoons olive oil

2 onions, cut into ¼" slices

2 zucchini, cut in half lengthwise,
    then cut into ¼" slices

2 yellow squash, cut in half lengthwise,
    then cut into ¼" slices

3 cloves garlic, finely chopped

½ cup white wine

   Salt

   Ground black pepper

¼ teaspoon Italian seasoning

Place the oil in a large saucepan over medium-high heat. Add the onions and cook for 3 to 5 minutes, or until translucent. Add the zucchini and the yellow squash, and cook for 4 to 5 minutes, stirring occasionally. Add the garlic, and cook for 30 seconds. Add the wine, salt and pepper to taste, and Italian seasoning. Cook for 2 to 3 minutes, or until the liquid has reduced by half.

Makes 4 servings

Per serving: *149 calories, 3 g protein, 15 g carbohydrate, 7 g fat, 0 mg cholesterol, 14 mg sodium, 5 g fiber*

Diet Exchanges: *0 milk, 3 vegetable, 0 fruit, 0 bread, 0 meat, 1½ fat*

1 Carb Choice

Creamy Mashed Cauliflower

102 Calories

—Mary Ann Tavares, Cumberland, Rhode Island

"This takes the place of mashed potatoes, and the whole family loves it as much as I do. They are all quite satisfied with the texture and taste."

Prep time: 7 minutes
Cook time: 25 minutes

1 head cauliflower, cut into florets, or
   1 bag (22 ounces) frozen cauliflower

1 teaspoon garlic powder

½ teaspoon salt

6 tablespoons reduced-fat cream cheese

1 tablespoon trans-free margarine

Bring a large saucepot of water to a boil. Add the cauliflower, and simmer for 25 minutes or until soft. (Follow the package directions if using frozen.) Drain and return the cauliflower to the pot. Add the garlic powder, salt, cream cheese, and margarine. Using a potato masher, mash the mixture until well combined. Serve warm.

Makes 5 servings

Per serving: *102 calories, 5 g protein, 8 g carbohydrate, 5 g fat, 10 mg cholesterol, 351 mg sodium, 3 g fiber*

Diet Exchanges: *0 milk, 1½ vegetable, 0 fruit, 0 bread, 0 meat, 1 fat*

½ Carb Choice

It Worked for Me!

Paula Gebhart

VITAL STATS

Weight lost: 60 pounds

Time to goal: Just under 1 year

Greatest challenge: Eating more fruits and vegetables

Paula Gebhart could have let time pack the pounds on, but she refused. After her kids entered school, she made the effort to get her weight under control. Now a fabulous role model for her children—and for adults—Paula continues to work at maintaining her weight by cooking healthy, nutritious meals and exercising frequently.

"As an 'early bloomer', I hit puberty at 11, and so always just felt heavier than the other girls. After college, I managed to drop about 15 pounds and felt really good about myself. It was at this time that I met my future husband. After we got married, however, I started putting the pounds back on.

"After the birth of my first child, I was unable to lose those last 15 pounds of baby weight. With my second pregnancy, I only gained a total of 25 pounds—but I never lost all of that, either. I was a stay-at-home mom, and also looked after other kids in my home, allowing me easy access to food throughout the day. Eventually, my weight hit 190 pounds;

at only 5'4", I couldn't keep fooling myself.

"The real issue for me was my children. I was very worried about embarrassing them when they entered school. So many mothers today are active, and I didn't want them to be the ones with the overweight mom. So I joined Weight Watchers. Their point-counting method was perfect for me because I have a problem with portion control; their approach helps me keep track of what and how much I am actually eating. I still use their program for maintenance, particularly when I find that I have gained a pound or two.

"I've changed the way I cook, frying less, eliminating the butter I used to use so generously, and staying aware of balance in each meal.

"I have to admit, however, that it is a little struggle every day. There are some days I don't want to stay on track, but all I have to do is think about the confidence I gained when I lost the weight. That great feeling is the inspiration that still keeps me going."

169 Calories

Lemon and Scallion Couscous

—Elizabeth Martlock, Jim Thorpe, Pennsylvania

Prep time: 8 minutes
Cook time: 10 minutes

  1 package (10 ounces) whole wheat couscous
  1 tablespoon olive oil
  1 clove garlic, finely chopped
 1½ cup reduced-sodium chicken broth
  2 teaspoons grated lemon zest
  2 tablespoons lemon juice
  ¼ cup white wine
  ¼ teaspoon salt
  1 bunch scallions, thinly sliced at an angle

Place the couscous in a large, heat-proof serving bowl.

In a large saucepan, heat the oil over medium-high heat. Add the garlic, and cook for 1 minute. Add the broth, lemon zest, lemon juice, wine, and salt. Bring to a boil, and cook for 2 minutes.

Pour the liquid mixture and scallions over the couscous, and cover. Let the mixture stand for about 5 minutes, or until the liquid has been absorbed, and fluff with a fork.

Makes 8 servings

Per serving: *169 calories, 6 g protein, 31 g carbohydrate, 3 g fat, 0 mg cholesterol, 89 mg sodium, 5 g fiber*

Diet Exchanges: *0 milk, 0 vegetable, 0 fruit, 2 bread, 0 meat, ½ fat*

2 Carb Choices

Snow Pea Sauté

—Melissa Sywensky, Macungie, Pennsylvania

"Along with providing lots of fiber and vitamins, veggies help you fill up and lose weight."

81 Calories

Prep time: 10 minutes
Cook time: 10 minutes

1 tablespoon olive oil
3 cloves garlic, finely chopped
1 pound snow peas, trimmed
  Salt (optional)
  Ground black pepper (optional)

In a large nonstick skillet, heat the oil over medium-high heat. Add the garlic, and cook for 3 minutes. Add the snow peas, tossing occasionally, and cook for 7 minutes, or until the snow peas turn bright green. Season to taste with salt and pepper, if using.

Makes 4 servings

Per serving: *81 calories, 3 g protein, 9 g carbohydrate, 4 g fat, 0 mg cholesterol, 5 mg sodium, 3 g fiber*

Diet Exchanges: *0 milk, 0 vegetable, 0 fruit, ½ bread, 0 meat, ½ fat*

½ Carb Choice

SECRETS OF WEIGHT-LOSS WINNERS

• Make your own trail mix to take everywhere with you—one for work, home, car, and so on—for those unannounced cravings.

—Priscilla Nanninga, Santa Maria, California

• I have a sweet tooth that won't quit. I've combined that trait with a limited budget to create a surefire diet tip: At the beginning of each month, I determine which foods I would like to limit. Typically, I say no cookies, candy, cake, or ice cream. If I eat the undesirable foods during the month, I must pay my two sons $20 each to blow on video games, CDs, or whatever they want. Knowing I can't afford to waste money that way has helped me to slip up only twice in 7 years!

—Bev Hill, Loomis, California

Main Dishes

SEAFOOD AND FISH

PORK

VEGETARIAN

285 Calories Incredible Meatloaf

—Gary Weller, Nelsonville, Ohio

*"I love meatloaf, so I found a great way to make it lower in fat.
Cutting out some of the carbs helped me lose weight, too."*

**Prep time: 5 minutes
Bake time: 55 to 65 minutes**

1½ **pounds 85% lean ground beef**
1 **cup cooked rice**
2 **tablespoons fat-free yogurt**
1 **rib celery, diced**
½ **medium onion, grated or diced**
Salt
Ground black pepper

Preheat the oven to 350°F. Coat a baking sheet with cooking spray.

In a large mixing bowl, mix together the beef, rice, yogurt, celery, onion, and salt and pepper to taste. Form into a loaf on the prepared baking sheet.

Bake for 55 to 65 minutes, or until a thermometer inserted in the center registers 160°F and the meat is no longer pink. Let stand for 10 minutes before slicing.

Makes 6 servings

Per serving: *285 calories, 22 g protein, 9 g carbohydrate, 17 g fat, 78 mg cholesterol, 88 mg sodium, 1 g fiber*

Diet Exchanges: *0 milk, 0 vegetable, 0 fruit, ½ bread, 3 meat, 0 fat*

1 Carb Choice

SHOPPING SAVVY
Olive Oil from Greece

Legend has it that olive oil was first produced thousands of years ago in the sun-drenched country of Greece. The same region that brings us this fruity oil has also brought us heart-healthy Mediterranean cuisine, in which olive oil plays an integral role. Terra Medi offers two extra virgin olive oils (one is organic). Both are made from Koroneiki olives grown in the balmy Peloponnesian peninsula, in southern Greece. Terra Medi olive oil is sold in attractive 17-ounce bottles at gourmet shops across the country. For a store near you, visit their Web site at www.terramedi.com.

Roast Beef with Caramelized Onion and Portabella Gravy

240 Calories

—**Elizabeth Martlock, Jim Thorpe, Pennsylvania**

Prep time: 10 minutes
Cook time: 1 hour 15 minutes
Stand time: 15 minutes

- 2 **pounds bottom round beef, trimmed of visible fat**
- 1 **teaspoon salt**
- ½ **teaspoon ground black pepper**
- 1 **clove garlic, minced**
- 1 **tablespoon olive oil**
- 6 **medium onions, thinly sliced**
- 2 **large cloves garlic, minced**
- 6 **cups sliced portabella mushrooms**
- 2 **cups reduced-sodium beef broth**
- 2 **tablespoons cornstarch**
- ¼ **cup water**
- **Salt**
- **Ground black pepper**
- 1 **bunch parsley, finely chopped**

Preheat the oven to 400°F. Coat the beef with cooking spray, then rub it with the salt, pepper, and garlic. Place the beef on a roasting pan with a rack, bake for 15 minutes, and then reduce the temperature to 350°F for 60 minutes, or until a thermometer inserted in the center registers 145°F for medium-rare, 160°F for medium, or 165°F for well-done. Let the meat stand for 15 minutes before carving to retain its juices.

Heat the oil in a large skillet over medium heat. Add the onions and cook for about 20 minutes or until they brown, stirring occasionally to avoid burning. Add the garlic and cook for about 1 minute. Add the mushrooms and cook for about 10 minutes, or until they're tender. Add the broth and bring to a boil.

In a small bowl, mix the cornstarch with the water, and whisk it into the mushroom mixture. Add salt and pepper to taste and allow the mixture to cook for an additional 5 minutes, cooking out the starch. Reduce the heat to low and cover, holding until the beef is ready.

After the beef has been carved, serve smothered with onion mushroom gravy. Garnish with parsley.

Makes 8 servings

Per serving: *240 calories, 29 g protein, 17 g carbohydrate, 7 g fat, 67 mg cholesterol, 480 mg sodium, 4 g fiber*

Diet Exchanges: *0 milk, 3 vegetable, 0 fruit, 0 bread, 4 meat, 1 fat*

1 Carb Choice

261 Calories

Chow Hound

—Jan Piacentini, Lake Orion, Michigan

"This recipe works well with ground turkey, too!"

Prep time: 12 minutes
Cook time: 18 minutes

1 pound 85% lean ground sirloin
　Salt
　Ground black pepper
1 medium sweet onion, chopped
1 red bell pepper, chopped
1 green bell pepper, chopped
1 cup fresh mushrooms, sliced
2 cups cooked white rice

In a large nonstick skillet over medium-high heat, cook the sirloin for 5 to 10 minutes or until it's browned, breaking it up with the back of a spoon as it cooks. Season to taste with salt and pepper.

Transfer the beef to a bowl and keep it warm. Drain all but 1 teaspoon of fat from the skillet before adding the onion, peppers, and mushrooms. Cook for 5 minutes, or until the vegetables are soft. Add the ground beef and rice to the skillet. Gently mix everything together until warmed throughout.

Makes 4 servings

Per serving: 261 calories, 26 g protein, 29 g carbohydrate, 5 g fat, 60 mg cholesterol, 71 mg sodium, 3 g fiber

Diet Exchanges: *0 milk, 1½ vegetable, 0 fruit, 1 bread, 3 meat, ½ fat*

2 Carb Choices

222 Calories

Healthy Shepherd's Pie

—Debra MacLean, Dartmouth, Nova Scotia, Canada

"This is a great recipe for weight loss since it has no white starches, such as potatoes, rice, or noodles, and it's low-fat and filling."

Prep time: 10 minutes
Cook time: 1 hour

1 **acorn squash**
½ **pound asparagus, trimmed and cut into 1" pieces**
1 **pound 90% extra-lean ground beef**
1 **cup frozen corn kernels**
1 **teaspoon onion powder**
Salt
Ground black pepper

Preheat the oven to 350°F. Coat a baking sheet and an 8" × 8" baking dish with cooking spray.

Slice the acorn squash in half lengthwise, and use a spoon to scrape out the seeds from its center. Lay the 2 halves face down on the prepared baking sheet and bake for 35 minutes, or until the squash is very tender. Remove from the oven and let rest for 10 to 15 minutes. Place a large nonstick skillet over medium-high heat and add the asparagus and ¼ cup of water. Cover and let the asparagus steam for 5 minutes, or until the asparagus is bright green. Use a slotted spoon to transfer the asparagus to a small bowl. Drain the pan and wipe it clean.

Brown the beef over medium heat in the same skillet you used for the asparagus, breaking it up with the back of a wooden spoon as it cooks. Remove the beef from the heat and drain any fat that has accumulated in the bottom of the pan. Add the corn and stir to combine. Season to taste with salt and pepper.

When the squash is cool enough to handle, scoop out the flesh with a spoon, and mash it with the back of a fork until it's smooth. Stir in the onion powder and season to taste with salt and pepper.

To assemble, spread half of the squash over the bottom of the casserole dish, followed by the ground beef mixture and then the asparagus. Top with the remaining squash. Bake uncovered for 20 minutes, or until warmed through.

Makes 4 servings

Per serving: *222 calories, 25 g protein, 22 g carbohydrate, 5 g fat, 60 mg cholesterol, 71 mg sodium, 4 g fiber*

Diet Exchanges: *0 milk, 2 vegetable, 0 fruit, ½ bread, 3 meat, 0 fat*

1½ Carb Choices

162
Calories

Phyllo Beef Pie

—Chris Detris, Breinigsville, Pennsylvania

Prep time: 20 minutes
Bake time: 15 minutes

1½ teaspoon canola oil
½ cup chopped mushrooms
½ large onion, chopped
1 medium carrot, shredded
1 rib celery, chopped
¼ teaspoon salt
3 tablespoons Dijon mustard
8 sheets phyllo dough, 17½" × 13"
⅓ cup trans-free margarine, melted
1 pound sliced rare deli roast beef
¾ cup shredded, reduced-fat Monterey Jack cheese

Heat the oven to 375°F.

In a 10" nonstick skillet, heat the oil over medium heat. When it's hot, add the mushrooms, onion, carrot, and celery. Cook for about 10 minutes, or until tender. Remove from the heat, and stir in the salt and 1 tablespoon of the mustard. Set aside.

Place one sheet of phyllo on your work surface (keep the rest covered with a damp towel so it won't dry out), and brush it with ½ tablespoon of the margarine. Top with another sheet of phyllo, brush it with margarine, and repeat to add two more sheets.

Cut the phyllo in half lengthwise, and then cut each half into 3 squares. Spread ½ teaspoon of mustard on the outer edges of each square. Repeat the entire process to make 6 more squares.

Divide the roast beef evenly on the phyllo squares. Spoon the vegetables over the beef and sprinkle them with the cheese. Bring the edges of dough up to form a package, and twist the top together. Brush each package with the remaining margarine. Place each package on a nonstick baking sheet and bake for 15 minutes, or until golden.

Makes 12 servings

Per serving: *162 calories, 11 g protein, 9 g carbohydrate, 9 g fat, 25 mg cholesterol, 529 mg sodium, 1 g fiber*

Diet Exchanges: *0 milk, 0 vegetable, 0 fruit, ½ bread, 1 meat, 1½ fat*

½ Carb Choice

It Worked for Me!

Christina Alderman

VITAL STATS

Weight lost: 140 pounds

Time to goal: About 1 year

Greatest challenge: Finally deciding to make a change

Christine started gaining weight in her early teens and hit 180 pounds by high school. At age 33, she decided to have weight-loss surgery. Not a "quick fix," the serious medical procedure led to permanent, positive life changes.

"In my junior year of high school, I gained 40 pounds. My family took notice, and my dad strongly urged me to lose weight. Always a 'people pleaser,' I tried every diet center around—but no luck. I felt pressure to be a good role model for my two younger siblings, making my failure to lose weight that much harder to bear.

"Ultimately, I got up to 300 pounds at age 33. Despite trying to eat 'right,' I still gained and gained. Then I saw a television program about Carnie Wilson and her surgery. That was my 'lightbulb' moment. I knew right then that I wanted to try the same solution.

Although my weight wasn't causing health problems at the time, I was afraid that if I waited too long I would develop diabetes or high blood pressure—or worse. I made up my mind in November and had the surgery in February. According to my doctors, I was the ideal candidate: I was at least 100 pounds overweight, motivated to follow their orders and to keep the weight off, and healthy enough to have this major procedure.

It may have been a quick decision, but it certainly wasn't easy. During surgery my spleen ruptured and had to be removed. Afterwards, I had two bouts with serious complications that kept me for extended hospital stays. But I never regretted any of it.

By Thanksgiving (9 months post-surgery), I'd lost 100 pounds. And now I've lost 140 pounds total, and kept it off. It's 5 years after the surgery, and I still can eat only very small amounts, although I do eat whatever kind of food I like. My relationship with food has changed dramatically; I attended the Culinary Institute of America and now work as a sous-chef supervisor in a hospital setting. I've always had an interest in food. Instead of a troubling issue, it is now a very healthy career.

Chicken Rolls with Cilantro Lime Pesto

—Mary Savannah, Butler, Pennsylvania

279 Calories

"This dish packs lots of flavor with very little fat. Enjoy!"

Prep time: 20 minutes
Cook time: 20 minutes

3 cloves garlic

½ small onion, chopped

½ cup cilantro

Juice of 1 lime

1 tablespoon marinated jalapeño chile peppers

4 boneless, skinless chicken breast halves (about 1½ pounds), butterflied and pounded to ¼" thick

Salt

Ground black pepper

1 tablespoon canola oil

½ cup shredded reduced-fat Monterey Jack or Cheddar cheese

In a blender or food processor, combine the garlic, onion, cilantro, lime juice, and peppers. Pulse for 4 or 5 seconds to blend.

Sprinkle the chicken breasts lightly with salt and pepper to taste. Spread ¼ of the garlic mixture over one side of each piece of chicken. Roll up the chicken and secure it with twine. Heat the oil in a large skillet over medium heat. When the oil is hot, add the chicken and cook for 10 to 15 minutes, turning to ensure that both sides are evenly browned. Remove the twine with kitchen scissors. Sprinkle each piece of chicken with the cheese just before serving.

Makes 4 servings

Per serving: *279 calories, 43 g protein, 4 g carbohydrate, 9 g fat, 109 mg cholesterol, 153 mg sodium, 1 g fiber*

Diet Exchanges: *0 milk, 0 vegetable, 0 fruit, 0 bread, 6 meat, 1 fat*

0 Carb Choice

Kitchen Tip

To butterfly a boneless chicken breast, start at the thickest side of the breast and slice it crosswise through the side, almost in half. Open the breast up like a book and press to flatten. To pound it thin, place the chicken between 2 pieces of plastic wrap and use the flat side of a meat mallet to pound it to the desired thickness, being careful not to tear the plastic.

Salsa Chicken Stir-Fry

—Allison Sommerville, Hamilton, Ontario, Canada

167 Calories

"This filling recipe is a good way to use up extra items in your fridge, since you can use other kinds of veggies if you want. I usually serve it over pasta or rice."

Prep time: 10 minutes
Cook time: 12 minutes

1 **pound boneless, skinless chicken breasts, cut into thin strips**
½ **onion, thinly sliced**
1 **clove garlic, minced**
½ **red pepper, thinly sliced**
1 **cup broccoli florets**
1 **cup salsa**
  Salt
  Ground black pepper
¼ **teaspoon ground red pepper (optional)**

In a large nonstick skillet over medium heat, cook the chicken, stirring frequently, until it is no longer pink and the juices run clear. Remove the chicken from the pan. In the same pan, cook the onion, garlic, pepper, and broccoli until crisp-tender. Return the chicken to the pan. Add the salsa and stir to coat. Cook for 1 or 2 minutes. Season to taste with salt, pepper, and red pepper, if using. Serve immediately.

Makes 4 servings

Per serving: *167 calories, 28 g protein, 8 g carbohydrate, 2 g fat, 66 mg cholesterol, 326 mg sodium, 2 g fiber*

Diet Exchanges: *0 milk, 1½ vegetable, 0 fruit, 0 bread, 4 meat, 0 fat*

½ **Carb Choice**

212 Calories

Chicken Poofs

—Tricia Andrews, Raleigh, North Carolina

Prep time: 15 minutes
Cook time: 14 minutes

- 1 cup reduced-sodium stuffing mix
- 1½ cups cooked chicken breast, chopped
- 1 cup fat-free sour cream
- 2 containers (8 rolls in each) reduced-fat crescent rolls
- Chicken gravy (optional)

Preheat the oven according to the directions on the crescent roll container.

In a medium saucepan, prepare the stuffing mix according to the package instructions. Remove it from the heat and mix in the chicken and sour cream.

On a large nonstick cookie sheet, unroll the crescent rolls. Separate them in pairs and arrange them to form four squares, pinching together the seams as you flatten the dough.

Place approximately ¾ cup of the stuffing mixture in the center of each square. Pull up the corners and make a pyramid of sorts with the crescent pastry. Pinch together all the seams, so you can't see any chicken mixture.

Bake for about 14 minutes, or until golden brown. Serve drizzled with hot chicken gravy, if using.

Makes 8 servings

Per serving: *212 calories, 13 g protein, 22 g carbohydrate, 7 g fat, 21 mg cholesterol, 335 mg sodium, 0 g fiber*

Diet Exchanges: *0 milk, 0 vegetable, 0 fruit, 1½ bread, 1½ meat, 1 fat*

1½ Carb Choices

Michelle's Roasted Chicken

—Michelle Schapker, Martinsville, Indiana

248 Calories

"I have been on a low-carb diet and have lost 65 pounds!
I don't cut all carbs because I know we need them, but eating
this chicken has helped me stay on a healthier diet."

Prep time: 15 minutes
Cook time: 1 hour 30 minutes

  1 **chicken, 3½–4 pounds, preferably free-range**
     Salt
     Ground black pepper
 ¼ **pound sliced prosciutto, cut into ½" pieces**
 ⅓ **cup shallots, minced**
  2 **cloves garlic, minced**
 ½ **cup whole green olives**
 ½ **cup white wine**

Preheat the oven to 350°F.

With a sharp, heavy knife, split the chicken down the backbone and open it up. Turn it breast side up and flatten with the palm of your hand. Cut a slit in the skin at the bottom of the breast and slip the "ankles" of the chicken through the slit. Sprinkle liberally with salt and pepper to taste. Transfer the chicken, breast side down, to a lightly oiled roasting pan. Bake for 45 minutes.

Meanwhile, in a mixing bowl, combine the prosciutto, shallots, garlic, and olives.

Remove the chicken from the oven and transfer it to a plate. Remove any accumulated fat from the roasting pan. Spread the prosciutto mixture evenly on the bottom of the roasting pan, and add the wine. Place the chicken into the pan, skin side up. Bake for 45 to 50 minutes longer, or until a thermometer inserted in a breast registers 180°F and the juices run clear.

Remove the chicken from the pan, and let it stand for 10 minutes before carving. Serve with the skin removed, topped with the prosciutto mixture.

Makes 4 servings

Per serving: *248 calories, 33 g protein, 6 g carbohydrate, 9 g fat, 105 mg cholesterol, 741 mg sodium, 0 g fiber*

Diet Exchanges: *0 milk, 1 vegetable, 0 fruit, 0 bread, 4 meat, 1 fat*

½ Carb Choice

Leni and Greg's One-Pan Chicken

—Steven Bloome, Mifflinburg, Pennsylvania

219 Calories

"This dish is very low in fat and carbs, but it's very filling and yummy. You can alter the taste to your liking. If carbs aren't an issue for you, it's delicious served over pasta or rice."

Prep time: 10 minutes
Cook time: 15 minutes

- 4 skinless, boneless, chicken breast halves, cut into 1" pieces
  Salt
  Ground black pepper
- 2 cloves garlic, minced
- 1 can (15 ounces) diced tomatoes, drained
- 1 bag (5 ounces) baby spinach
- 2 cups thinly sliced mushrooms
- ½ cup Parmesan cheese, grated

Season the chicken with salt and pepper to taste.

Coat a large nonstick skillet with cooking spray, and place it over medium heat. When it's hot, add the chicken and cook for 5 to 10 minutes, or until it's no longer pink and the juices run clear.

Remove the chicken to a plate, covering to keep it warm. Add the garlic to the pan. Cook for 2 to 3 minutes, or until the garlic is fragrant. Add the tomatoes, spinach, and mushrooms. Cook for about 3 minutes, or until the liquid is reduced by half. Put the chicken back in the pan and stir. Adjust the seasoning, if necessary. Sprinkle with the cheese just before serving.

Makes 4 servings, 1 cup each

Per serving: *219 calories, 34 g protein, 11 g carbohydrate, 5 g fat, 75 mg cholesterol, 432 mg sodium, 2 g fiber*

Diet Exchanges: *0 milk, 2 vegetable, 0 fruit, 0 bread, 4½ meat, 0 fat*

1 Carb Choice

Ted's Seasoned Chicken Skewers

—Ted Kranenberg, Cambridge, Minnesota

143 Calories

Prep time: 35 minutes
Marinate time: 30 minutes
Cook time: 6 minutes

2 large Yukon Gold or sweet potatoes, unpeeled and cut into thirds

Juice of 2 lemons

⅓ cup extra virgin olive oil

4 cloves garlic, minced

1 teaspoon ground rosemary

Salt

Ground black pepper

4 boneless, skinless chicken breast halves, cut into 1" pieces

1 pint of cherry tomatoes

20 bamboo skewers, each 8" long, soaked in water for 30 minutes and drained

Place the potatoes in a medium pot, and add enough water to cover them. Place the pot over high heat and bring to a boil for 5 minutes. Drain the potatoes. When they're cool enough to handle, cut them into 1" pieces.

In a medium bowl, combine the lemon juice, olive oil, garlic, and rosemary. Season with salt and pepper to taste. Add the chicken and the potatoes. Toss lightly to coat. Let the mixture marinate in the refrigerator for at least 30 minutes, preferably overnight.

Preheat the grill to high. Thread the chicken, potatoes, and cherry tomatoes onto the skewers, alternating ingredients. Grill each skewer for 2 to 3 minutes on each side, or until the chicken is no longer pink and the juices run clear.

Makes 10 servings

Per serving: *143 calories, 12 g protein, 10 g carbohydrate, 6 g fat, 26 mg cholesterol, 34 mg sodium, 2 g fiber*

Diet Exchanges: *0 milk, ½ vegetable, 0 fruit, ½ bread, 1½ meat, 1 fat*

1 Carb Choice

Chicken Stroganoff with Broccoli

320 Calories

—Suzanne Hasmanis, Lawrenceville, Georgia

"This recipe offers plenty of protein and vitamins and keeps your carbohydrate intake to a minimum. Sprinkle some ground flaxseed on top, and you've added extra fiber to round out your meal. Enjoy!"

Prep time: 15 minutes
Cook time: 20 minutes

- 2 boneless, skinless chicken breasts, cooked and cut up into bite-size pieces
- 1 container (16 ounces) fat-free sour cream
- 1 can (10½ ounces) fat-free cream of chicken soup
- 1 can (8 ounces) canned mushrooms, sliced
- ½ teaspoon salt
- ¼ teaspoon ground black pepper
- 1 teaspoon parsley flakes
- 2 heads broccoli, cut into florets

In a large saucepan over medium-high heat, combine the chicken, sour cream, soup, mushrooms, salt, pepper, and parsley. Simmer for about 20 minutes, or until the sauce thins out. Steam the broccoli for about 3 minutes, or until crisp-tender. Serve the chicken over the broccoli.

Makes 4 servings

Per serving: *320 calories, 32 g protein, 32 g carbohydrate, 8 g fat, 56 mg cholesterol, 1002 mg sodium, 5 g fiber*

Diet Exchanges: *0 milk, 4 vegetable, 0 fruit, ½ bread, 3 meat, 1 fat*

2 Carb Choices

Chicken Teriyaki and Brown Rice

—Kerri Kerichenko, Chicopee, Massachusetts

169 Calories

"It's a great meal that fills you up quickly."

Prep time: 5 minutes
Cook time: 20 minutes

¼ cup long grain rice

1 pound boneless, skinless chicken breasts, cut into 1" cubes

1 package (16 ounces) frozen mixed vegetables, thawed

1 teaspoon cornstarch

½ cup low-sodium chicken broth

¼ cup teriyaki sauce

Cook the rice according to the package directions, and set it aside. Meanwhile, coat a large nonstick saucepan with cooking spray and place it over medium-high heat. Add the chicken, and cook for 6 to 7 minutes, or until brown. Add the vegetables, and cook for 5 to 10 minutes, or until the vegetables are heated through.

In a small bowl, whisk the cornstarch into the broth until dissolved. Add the teriyaki sauce. Add to the chicken mixture. Bring to a boil for 1 minute, and remove from the heat.

Combine the rice with the chicken mixture to serve.

Makes 6 servings

Per serving: *169 calories, 21 g protein, 17 g carbohydrate, 1 g fat, 44 mg cholesterol, 623 mg sodium, 3 g fiber*

Diet Exchanges: *0 milk, ½ vegetable, 0 fruit, 1 bread, 2½ meat, 0 fat*

1 Carb Choice

352
Calories

Speedy Chicken

—Linda Chaput, Rutherglen, Ontario, Canada

Prep time: 5 minutes
Cook time: 45 minutes

2 chicken breasts and 2 chicken thighs, skin removed
¼ cup ketchup
¼ cup mustard
¼ cup brown sugar
1 teaspoon chili powder

Preheat the oven to 350°F. Coat a baking dish with cooking spray and arrange chicken in it.

In a small bowl, mix together the ketchup, mustard, brown sugar, and chili powder. Pour over the chicken and bake, uncovered, for 45 to 60 minutes, or until the internal temperature reaches 170°F.

Makes 2 servings

Per serving: *352 calories, 44 g protein, 29 g carbohydrate, 7 g fat, 126 mg cholesterol, 825 mg sodium, 1 g fiber*

Diet Exchanges: *0 milk, 0 vegetable, 0 fruit, 2 bread, 6 meat, 1 fat*

2 Carb Choices

⋯⋯ SECRETS OF WEIGHT-LOSS WINNERS ⋯⋯

• Sit down once a week and look through your recipes. Pick out six or seven healthy meals and shop for the items you need. This makes cooking dinner wonderful because you already know ahead of time what you'll be cooking on what nights, and you will have everything that you need.

—Hope Lewis, Bartlett, Tennessee

• Play outside with your kids! It's great for you and for them.

—Michael Turton, Ft. Mitchell, Kentucky

• Reward your dieting efforts in non-food ways. Treat yourself to a pedicure, manicure, or massage.

—Nancy Roth, Saint Joseph, Illinois

• Brush your teeth and apply tooth-whitening solution around the time you want to stop eating for the night. This guarantees that you won't snack before bedtime and helps your appearance in more ways than one!

—Kelly Kennedy, Edmonton, Alberta, Canada

Delicious Dill Chicken

—Christine Olliffe, Tavistock, Ontario, Canada

136 Calories

"This is a tasty recipe that my family loves. It's easy to make, and because it's skinless, there's less fat!"

Prep time: 10 minutes
Cook time: 30 minutes

2 tablespoons minced fresh dill

2 tablespoons Worcestershire sauce

½ teaspoon soy sauce

¼ cup finely chopped Spanish onion

¼ teaspoon ground black pepper

4 boneless, skinless chicken breast halves

In a resealable plastic bag, combine the dill, Worcestershire sauce, soy sauce, onion, and pepper. Add the chicken and gently massage the ingredients in the closed bag. Refrigerate for at least 30 minutes, preferably overnight.

Preheat the oven to 350°F. Coat a 9" × 9" baking dish with cooking spray and place the chicken and marinade in it. Bake, uncovered, for 20 to 30 minutes, or until a thermometer inserted into the thickest part of the chicken registers 160°F and the juices run clear.

Makes 4 servings

Per serving: *136 calories, 25 g protein, 3 g carbohydrate, 2 g fat, 65 mg cholesterol, 204 mg sodium, 0 g fiber*

Diet Exchanges: *0 milk, ½ vegetable, 0 fruit, 0 bread, 3 meat, 0 fat*

0 Carb Choice

Madras Orange Chicken with Ginger Fried Rice

—Elaine Sweet, Dallas, Texas

"This light and healthful recipe is full of flavor. The chicken is especially tender and delicious. The tantalizing flavors really fill you up!"

589 Calories

Prep time: 35 minutes
Cook time: 20 minutes

CHICKEN

- 4 boneless, skinless chicken breasts (4 ounces each), rinsed and blotted dry
- 1 teaspoon sesame oil
- 1 tablespoon Madras curry powder
- ½ cup orange juice
- ½ teaspoon red pepper flakes
- 1 cup chopped pineapple
- ½ cup orange segments, seeded and chopped
- ½ cup chopped red bell pepper
- ½ cup finely chopped onion
- ½ cup light coconut milk

RICE

- ½ tablespoon sesame oil
- 2 cloves garlic, finely chopped
- ¾ tablespoon finely chopped crystallized ginger
- 5 scallions, finely sliced
- 2 tablespoons chopped red bell pepper
- 1½ cups uncooked rice
- 2 tablespoons tamari
- 2 tablespoons brown sugar
- 2 tablespoons rice vinegar
- 3 cups hot water

To make the chicken: Place the chicken in a bowl. Combine the oil, curry powder, orange juice, and red pepper flakes. Pour over the chicken. Marinate in the refrigerator for 20 minutes.

Coat a large nonstick skillet with cooking spray. Remove the chicken from the marinade, reserving the marinade. Cook the chicken over medium-high heat for 10 minutes.

Remove the chicken from the skillet and cover it with aluminum foil. Add the pineapple, orange segments, bell pepper, and onion to the skillet. Cook for about 5 minutes, or until the pepper is cooked. Add the coconut milk and the reserved marinade. Bring to a boil. Reduce the heat and let it simmer for 5 minutes. Return the chicken to the skillet.

To make the rice: Heat the oil in a large skillet over medium-high heat. Add the garlic, ginger, and scallions. Cook for 2 to 3 minutes, or until the vegetables are aromatic. Add the pepper. Cook for another minute. Add the rice, tamari, sugar, vinegar, and water. Cook for another 18 to 20 minutes, or until the rice is tender. Serve with the chicken.

Makes 4 servings

Per serving: *589 calories, 36 g protein, 88 g carbohydrate, 12 g fat, 68 mg cholesterol, 748 mg sodium, 5 g fiber*

Diet Exchanges: *0 milk, 1 vegetable, 1 fruit, 4 bread, 4 meat, 2 fat*

6 Carb Choices

It Worked for Me!

Linda Lindsey

VITAL STATS

Weight lost: 100 pounds

Time to goal: 2 years

Greatest challenge: Ending the cycle of using food as the solution to every problem

Linda Lindsey had a tough start in life. Sexually abused as a young girl, she used weight gain as a way to shield herself from unwanted physical attention. When she reached adulthood, Linda worked with a therapist to understand her troubled relationship with food, and the pounds finally started to come off.

"Starting at about 9 years old, I learned to eat for all the wrong reasons. I was eating for comfort, eating for control—I ate for any reason other than actually needing fuel. I started gaining and never looked back. My parents urged me to try every diet out there. When I was 12, they enrolled me in Nutrisystem (I think I was the youngest person ever accepted into that program at the time). But nothing worked.

"At age 25, I visited my doctor for an ingrown toenail. He mentioned that I had gained weight and that he wanted me to step on a scale—but we had to use the hay baling scale at the farm next door. I will never forget seeing '306' flashing at me in big red numbers. He sent me to a nutritionist. I was able to lose 100 pounds, mostly by eliminating the nine cans of soda I drank each day and shaving off 1,000 calories per week.

"Despite the substantial weight loss, however, I never addressed why I had been overeating in the first place. Over the following year, I gained back 70 pounds and started to wonder just what was wrong with me.

"But then, I found my way to a therapist. I sat down and literally said, 'Look, my job is fine, my friends are fine—I only want to talk about my weight, please don't let me talk about anything else.' With her guidance, I addressed powerfully painful issues from my childhood, including abuse and feelings of abandonment. I lost 140 pounds and got down to a size 10.

"I am now a motivational speaker and author of a website called www.facethefat.com. I help others realize that they can stop choosing to be overweight. Once you remember that food is fuel, you can stop choosing to overeat—and you will lose weight."

249 Calories

Low-Carb Nutty Chicken

—Susan Jerrott, Bedford, Nova Scotia, Canada

"This dish is delicious and very low-carb. I eat it with a Caesar salad for a low-carb meal and it has helped me lose lots of weight."

Prep time: 30 minutes
Marinate time: 1 hour
Cook time: 10 to 12 minutes

 3 tablespoons soy sauce
 2 tablespoons rice wine
 3 tablespoons chicken broth
 1 teaspoon sugar substitute
2½ tablespoons minced gingerroot
 3 cloves garlic, minced
 1 pound chicken tenders
 1 egg
 ½ teaspoon water
 ¾ cup almonds, ground

Preheat the oven to 375°F.

Coat a baking sheet with cooking spray. In a resealable plastic bag, combine the soy sauce, rice wine, broth, sugar substitute, ginger, and garlic. Shake to combine. Place the chicken in the bag of marinade, and coat. Marinate in the refrigerator for at least 1 hour, turning the chicken after 30 minutes. Remove the chicken from the marinade and drain it on a paper towel. In a flat bowl, beat the egg lightly with the water. Dip each piece of chicken in the egg mixture, and roll them in the almonds to coat. Let the almond-coated pieces set for 15 minutes. Arrange them on the baking sheet, and bake for 5 to 6 minutes per batch.

Makes 4 servings

Per serving: *249 calories, 32 g protein, 6 g carbohydrate, 11 g fat, 120 mg cholesterol, 879 mg sodium, 2 g fiber*

Diet Exchanges: *0 milk, 0 vegetable, 0 fruit, ½ bread, 4 meat, 2 fat*

½ Carb Choice

249 Calories

Spicy Baked Chicken

—Rosalind Rauschenberg, Blountstown, Florida

"You will not only lose weight eating this low-fat recipe, you will also love the way it tastes! What more could anyone want?"

Prep time: 10 minutes
Cook time: 1 hour

  4 **skinless chicken leg quarters**
      Salt
      Ground black pepper
1½ **cups barbecue sauce**
  1 **medium onion, chopped**
  1 **medium green bell pepper, chopped**

Preheat the oven to 400°F. Coat a roasting pan with nonstick cooking spray.

Place the chicken in the pan. Sprinkle with salt and pepper to taste. Pour the barbecue sauce over the chicken and arrange the onion and bell pepper on top. Cover the pan with aluminum foil and bake for 1 hour, or until a thermometer inserted into the thickest part of the chicken registers 160°F and the juices run clear.

Makes 4 servings

Per serving: *249 calories, 29 g protein, 17 g carbohydrate, 7 g fat, 104 mg cholesterol, 877 mg sodium, 2 g fiber*

Diet Exchanges: *0 milk, 1 vegetable, 0 fruit, 1 bread, 3½ meat, 1 fat*

1 Carb Choice

Stuffed Southwestern Chicken Breasts

376 Calories

—Theresa Wagner, Florida, New York

Prep time: 15 minutes
Cook time: 25 minutes

- 1 **cup cooked, reduced-sodium, Spanish-style rice**
- ¼ **cup green onions, thinly sliced**
- ⅛ **teaspoon ground black pepper**
- 4 **skinless, boneless chicken breast halves, about 1½ pounds total, butterflied and pounded to ¼" thick (see "Kitchen Tip" on page 126)**
- ½ **cup dry bread crumbs**
- ¼ **cup grated Parmesan cheese**
- ½ **teaspoon chili powder**
- ½ **teaspoon garlic salt**
- ¼ **teaspoon ground cumin**
- ¼ **teaspoon trans-free margarine, melted**

Preheat the oven to 400°F.

In a medium bowl, combine the rice, green onions, and black pepper. Place about a ¼ cup of the mixture in the center of each chicken breast; roll the breasts up, tuck the ends under, and secure them with twine.

In a shallow baking dish, combine the bread crumbs, cheese, chili powder, garlic salt, and cumin, and stir to blend well. Roll the chicken bundles in the margarine, and then in the crumb mixture. Place them seam side down in a 13" × 9" baking dish.

Bake, uncovered, for 15 to 20 minutes, or until the chicken is cooked through. Remove the twine before serving.

Makes 4 servings

Per serving: *376 calories, 46 g protein, 32 g carbohydrate, 6 g fat, 103 mg cholesterol, 596 mg sodium, 1 g fiber*

Diet Exchanges: *0 milk, 0 vegetable, 0 fruit, 2 bread, 6 meat, 0 fat*

2 Carb Choices

Chicken Balsamico with Pears

—Menote Caires, Wayne, New Jersey

"This kind of recipe is easy, tasty, and healthy. It is this kind of food that keeps my taste buds happy while allowing me to lose weight."

271 Calories

Prep time: 10 minutes
Cook time: 15 to 20 minutes

- 4 boneless, skinless chicken breast halves
  Salt
  Ground black pepper
- 1 tablespoon extra-virgin olive oil
- 2 garlic cloves, chopped
- 2 medium Bosc pears, peeled, cored, and sliced
- 1 cup reduced-sodium chicken broth
- ¼ cup balsamic vinegar
- 1½ tablespoons honey
- 1½ teaspoons cornstarch

Rinse the chicken in cold water. Then pat dry with paper towels. Place each chicken breast half between two sheets of plastic wrap and pound the chicken breasts to ½" thick. Remove the plastic and sprinkle both sides of each breast with salt and pepper to taste.

In a large skillet over medium-high heat, heat the oil. Add the chicken and cook for 3 to 4 minutes on each side, turning once, until it's no longer pink in the center and the juices run clear. Remove the chicken from the heat and transfer it to a platter. Cover it to keep it warm.

Add the garlic and turn the heat down to medium for 2 minutes, or until the garlic is soft. Add the pears and continue cooking for 3 to 4 minutes, stirring occasionally, until the pears are soft and golden brown.

In a small bowl, combine the chicken broth, balsamic vinegar, honey, and cornstarch. Pour over the pear mixture. Increase the heat to high until it comes to a boil, and then immediately lower the heat and simmer, stirring frequently for 4 to 6 minutes, or until the sauce thickens slightly. Return the chicken and any juices to the pan and cook for 1 to 2 minutes. Taste and adjust the seasoning, if necessary.

Place the chicken on individual serving plates or on a large platter. Use a slotted spoon to mound the fruit over the top. Spoon the sauce over the fruit and around the chicken. Serve immediately.

Makes 4 servings

Per serving: *271 calories, 28 g protein, 27 g carbohydrate, 6 g fat, 66 mg cholesterol, 101 mg sodium, 3 g fiber*

Diet Exchanges: *0 milk, 0 vegetable, 1 fruit, 1 bread, 4 meat, 1 fat*

2 Carb Choices

335 Calories

Chicken in a Pot

—Igor Blahut, Glen Allen, Virginia

Prep time: 20 minutes
Cook time: 1 hour 15 minutes

10 black peppercorns

4 whole allspice

4 sprigs thyme

1 bay leaf

10 small red potatoes (about 1 pound)

5 carrots, cut into 1"-thick pieces

2 leeks, trimmed and cut into 3 pieces each

2 onions, quartered

3 cans (16 ounces each) fat-free, reduced-sodium chicken broth

1 chicken (about 3 pounds)

1½ tablespoons trans-free butter or margarine

2 tablespoons unbleached or all-purpose flour

½ cup 2% milk

Salt

Ground black pepper

2 tablespoons minced fresh chives (optional)

Place the peppercorns, allspice, thyme, and bay leaf in a piece of cheesecloth. Gather the edges of the cheesecloth together, and tie it with twine into a small bag. In a large saucepot over medium-high heat, place the cheesecloth, potatoes, carrots, leeks, onions, chicken broth, and chicken. Bring to a boil, then reduce the heat, and simmer uncovered for 25 minutes. Turn the chicken over and cook for 20 minutes more, or until the internal temperature of the chicken registers 170°F on an instant-read thermometer and the vegetables are tender.

Remove the chicken and vegetables with a slotted spoon. Set them aside, and keep them warm. Discard the cheesecloth bag. Return the broth to a boil, and cook for about 15 minutes, or until it's reduced to 4 cups. Remove from the heat.

Melt the butter in a saucepan over medium heat. Stir in the flour, reduce the heat, and cook for 1 minute, stirring constantly with a wooden spoon. Whisk in 1 cup of the broth mixture, reserving the remaining broth for future use. (See "Kitchen Tip," opposite page.) Whisk in the milk. Cook, stirring frequently, for about 8 minutes, or until the broth thickens. Adjust the taste with salt and black pepper.

Remove the chicken meat from its bones and discard the bones and the skin. Chop the chicken into small pieces. Arrange the reserved vegetables on a platter, and top with the chopped chicken. Spoon the sauce over the chicken and vegetables. Sprinkle with chives, if using.

Makes 6 servings

Per serving: *335 calories, 30 g protein, 32 g carbohydrate, 10 g fat, 79 mg cholesterol, 847 mg sodium, 5 g fiber*

Diet Exchanges: *0 milk, 3 vegetable, 0 fruit, 1 bread, 3½ meat, 2 fat*

2 Carb Choices

Kitchen Tip

To save the extra stock generated by this recipe, first transfer it to a covered container and refrigerate it until chilled. The fat will congeal on the surface and can then be easily removed. To make easy-to-use portions, freeze the stock in a muffin pan or ice cube tray. Once the portions are frozen, pop them out and store them in a resealable freezer bag for up to 6 months.

288 Calories

Thai Stir-Fry

—Kelly Bishop, Winnipeg, Manitoba, Canada

"This recipe has lots of healthy vegetables and tons of flavor and heat from the Thai peanut sauce."

Prep time: 12 minutes
Cook time: 15 minutes

2 tablespoons sunflower oil

2 boneless, skinless chicken breast halves, cut into thin strips

3 cloves garlic, crushed

½ medium onion, thinly sliced

1 cup broccoli florets

1 carrot, thinly sliced

½ red or yellow pepper, sliced

1½ cups snow peas or snap peas

½ cup thinly sliced bok choy

1 cup prepared Thai-style peanut sauce

1 package (12 ounces) rice vermicelli noodles

1 cup bean sprouts

½ cup unsalted peanuts (optional)

In a large nonstick skillet over medium-high heat, warm the oil. Add the chicken and cook, stirring frequently, for 5 minutes, or until the chicken is no longer pink and the juices run clear. Add the garlic and onion, and cook until the onion is fragrant. Add the broccoli, carrot, pepper, snow peas, and bok choy. Cook for about 10 minutes, or until the vegetables are bright and crisp-tender. Transfer to a large bowl, and toss with the peanut sauce.

Meanwhile, soak the noodles in hot water for 5 minutes. Drain the noodles and add them to the chicken and vegetables. Add the bean sprouts and toss gently to coat. Top with the peanuts, if using.

Makes 8 servings

Per serving: *288 calories, 14 g protein, 31 g carbohydrate, 12 g fat, 16 mg cholesterol, 110 mg sodium, 3 g fiber*

Diet Exchanges: *0 milk, ½ vegetable, 0 fruit, 1½ bread, 1½ meat, 2 fat*

2 Carb Choices

Ranch Baked Salmon with Pilaf

—Jeo Oiesen, Taos, New Mexico

368 Calories

"Since getting married less than 2 years ago, my husband has lost 85 pounds and has been amazed at how good dishes like this taste."

Prep time: 5 minutes
Cook time: 15 minutes

½ **pound salmon fillets**
2 **teaspoons trans-free margarine**
1¼ **teaspoons minced garlic**
2 **tablespoons fat-free ranch dressing**
¼ **teaspoon lemon-herb seasoning**
  Ground black pepper
¼ **cup quick-cooking brown rice**
½ **cup sliced mushrooms**
1 **cup Asian-style frozen vegetable mix**
1 **green onion, thinly sliced**
1 **tablespoon sliced almonds**

Preheat the oven to 400°F. Coat an 8" × 8" baking dish with cooking spray.

Rinse and dry the salmon and arrange the fillets skin-side down in the prepared baking dish. Spread 1 teaspoon of margarine on each salmon fillet. Sprinkle the fillets with ¼ teaspoon of the garlic, followed by the ranch dressing. Top by sprinkling with lemon-herb seasoning and pepper to taste. Bake for 15 minutes, or until the thickest part of the fillet flakes easily with a fork.

While the salmon is baking, cook the rice according to the package directions, and set it aside. While the rice is cooking, heat a non-stick skillet over medium heat and cook the mushrooms, vegetable mix, and the remaining garlic for 5 minutes, or until soft. Add the vegetable mixture to the cooked rice, along with the green onion and almonds, and stir to combine well. Cover and keep warm. Serve with the salmon.

Makes 2 servings

Per serving: *368 calories, 27 g protein, 23 g carbohydrate, 19 g fat, 67 mg cholesterol, 572 mg sodium, 2 g fiber*

Diet Exchanges: *0 milk, 1½ vegetable, 0 fruit, 1 bread, 3 meat, 2 fat*

1½ Carb Choices

Pasta with Shellfish and Mushrooms

—Elaine Beierbach, Medicine Hat, Alberta, Canada

480 Calories

"This dish is simple to make and tasty, as well as healthy. It tastes like a gourmet dish even though it is relatively inexpensive to prepare."

Prep time: 10 minutes
Cook time: 15 minutes

1 tablespoon olive oil

1 tin (10 ounces) baby clams, with juice

1 pound shrimp, peeled and deveined

2 cups sliced mushrooms

2 large tomatoes, peeled and coarsely chopped

2 cloves garlic, minced

1 tablespoon fresh dill or 1 teaspoon dried dill, + additional for garnish (optional)

Salt

Ground black pepper

8 ounces whole wheat linguine

⅓ cup grated Parmesan cheese

Warm the oil in a large saucepan over medium-high heat. When it's hot, add the clams, shrimp, and mushrooms. Cook, stirring occasionally, for about 5 minutes, or until the shrimp are pink and the mushrooms are soft. Add the tomatoes, garlic, and dill. Reduce the heat to low and simmer for about 10 minutes, or until the juice from the tomatoes evaporates a bit. Season to taste with the salt and pepper.

Meanwhile, in a large pot, cook the linguine according to package directions. Drain the pasta and place it in a large bowl. Add the shellfish mixture and toss gently to combine. Sprinkle with the cheese and additional dill, if using, and serve.

Makes 4 servings

Per serving: *480 calories, 46 g protein, 51 g carbohydrate, 11 g fat, 235 mg cholesterol, 645 mg sodium, 3 g fiber*

Diet Exchanges: *0 milk, 1 vegetable, 0 fruit, 2½ bread, 5 meat, 1 fat*

3 Carb Choices

Kitchen Tip

If you blanch your tomatoes, their skins will slip off easily. Begin by coring the tomatoes with a paring knife, removing the stems and white middles. Then cut an X in the bottom of each tomato, cutting only the skin. Bring a pot of water to a boil and add the tomatoes to the water. Boil for about 30 seconds. Remove the tomatoes from the pot and immediately plunge them into ice water to stop the cooking process. When the tomatoes are cool enough to handle, use the edge of the knife to slip off the skin.

Crunchy Baked Cod with Sun-Dried Tomato Sauce

203 Calories

—Ranee Solomon, Akron, Ohio

"This is an easy and delicious low-carb main dish! The crunch of the almonds gives it just the right touch."

Prep time: 5 minutes
Cook time: 20 minutes

¼ cup sun-dried tomatoes
¼ cup almonds
½ cup low-carb bread crumbs
⅓ cup reduced-fat mayonnaise
  Salt
  Ground black pepper
1 pound cod fillets, fresh or frozen, thawed

Preheat the oven to 425°F. Coat a baking sheet with cooking spray.

Soak the sun-dried tomatoes in ¼ cup of hot water until they are soft enough to chop.

Meanwhile, pulse the almonds in a food processor until they're finely ground. Transfer to a small bowl and toss with the bread crumbs. Set aside.

Combine the tomatoes and mayonnaise in a food processor, and pulse until smooth. Add salt and pepper to taste.

Arrange the cod on the prepared baking sheet. Spread the mayonnaise mixture evenly over the fish. Sprinkle with the almond mixture. Cook for 20 minutes, or until the fish flakes easily.

Makes 4 servings

Per serving: *203 calories, 24 g protein, 9 g carbohydrate, 8 g fat, 42 mg cholesterol, 355 mg sodium, 2 g fiber*

Diet Exchanges: *0 milk, ½ vegetable, 0 fruit, ½ bread, 3 meat, 1 fat*

1 Carb Choice

124
Calories

Zesty Baked Fish

—Phyllis LaCroix, West Union, Illinois

"I am not a big fan of fish, but this fish is so yummy.
You can use cod in place of the orange roughy, if you prefer."

Prep time: 5 minutes
Cook time: 15 minutes

  1 **pound orange roughy fillets**
  ⅓ **cup reduced-fat mayonnaise**
  2 **tablespoons grated Parmesan cheese**
  1 **scallion, thinly sliced**
  ½ **teaspoon Worcestershire sauce**

Preheat the oven to 450°F.

Coat a 9" × 13" baking pan with nonstick cooking spray and arrange the fillets in the pan.

In a small bowl, stir together the mayonnaise, cheese, scallion, and Worcestershire sauce. Spread the mixture over the fish fillets.

Bake uncovered for 15 minutes, or until the fish flakes easily with a fork.

Makes 4 servings

Per serving: *124 calories, 18 g protein, 3 g carbohydrate, 4 g fat, 25 mg cholesterol, 289 mg sodium, 0 g fiber*

Diet Exchanges: *0 milk, 0 vegetable, 0 fruit, 0 bread, 2½ meat, ½ fat*

0 Carb Choice

Marinated Shrimp with Ginger, Lime, Cilantro, and Honey

42 Calories

—Patricia Naveira, Burbank, California

"I like knowing I can grab some of this shrimp as a protein pick-me-up, since there is no oil to worry about."

Prep time: 10 minutes
Chill time: 4 hours

   Juice of 2 limes
1 tablespoon Dijon mustard
1 teaspoon finely grated ginger
1 tablespoon honey
¼ cup chopped cilantro
2 scallions, white part only, sliced
2 pounds (about 36) large shrimp, cooked
8 cups mixed salad greens (optional)

In a small bowl, whisk together the lime juice, mustard, ginger, and honey. Add the cilantro and scallions. Place the shrimp in a large, resealable plastic bag. Pour the lime juice mixture over the shrimp, coating them completely. Let the shrimp marinate in the refrigerator for at least 4 hours, preferably overnight. Serve chilled over a bed of the salad greens, if using.

Makes 8 servings

Per serving: *42 calories, 5 g protein, 5 g carbohydrate, .5 g fat, 48 mg cholesterol, 103 mg sodium, 1 g fiber*

Diet Exchanges: *0 milk, 0 vegetable, 0 fruit, ½ bread, 1 meat, 0 fat*

½ Carb Choice

358 Calories

Oven-Fried Catfish Provençal

—Lillian Julow, Gainesville, Florida

"This oven-baked dish has a lot fewer calories than the fried version. The flavors are just as delicious."

Prep time: 8 minutes
Chill time: 15 minutes
Cook time: 15 minutes

- ¼ cup fat-free half-and-half
- 1 tablespoon Dijon mustard
- ¼ teaspoon salt
- ¼ teaspoon ground black pepper
  Pinch dried rosemary
- ¼ cup dry bread crumbs
- 2 tablespoons grated fresh Parmesan cheese
- 2 pounds catfish fillets

Preheat the oven to 400°F. Lightly coat a baking sheet with cooking spray, and set it aside.

In a small microwaveable bowl, combine 1 tablespoon of the half-and-half with the mustard, salt, pepper, and rosemary. Set aside.

Place the remaining half-and-half in a shallow bowl. In another shallow bowl, combine the bread crumbs and Parmesan cheese. Dip each piece of catfish in the half-and-half and then dredge each one in the bread crumb mixture, arranging them in one layer on the prepared baking sheet.

Refrigerate the catfish for 15 minutes to set the crumbs, and then bake for 15 minutes, or until the fillets flake easily.

When the fish is done, microwave the reserved cream mixture on high for 20 seconds, or until it's warm. Drizzle over the fillets just before serving.

Makes 4 servings

Per serving: *358 calories, 37 g protein, 7 g carbohydrate, 17 g fat, 110 mg cholesterol, 473 mg sodium, 0 g fiber*

Diet Exchanges: *0 milk, 0 vegetable, 0 fruit, ½ bread, 5 meat, 1 fat*

½ Carb Choice

Shrimp and Vegetable Pasta

—Janet English, Toronto, Ontario, Canada

388 Calories

"This recipe is chock-full of hearty vegetables and protein-packed shrimp, as well as nutritious whole wheat pasta! This meal is healthy, filling, and full of fiber and vitamins. It satisfies every taste bud and usually keeps me satisfied so that I do not crave sweet desserts."

Prep time: 10 minutes
Cook time: 12 minutes

1 tablespoon olive oil

1 clove garlic, chopped

1 small onion, diced

½ green bell pepper, thinly sliced

1 cup thinly sliced mushrooms

1 cup sliced zucchini

Salt

Ground black pepper

1 can (15 ounces) Italian-style diced tomatoes

1 pound medium shrimp, peeled and deveined

1 teaspoon dried oregano

½ teaspoon dried basil

½ teaspoon dried thyme

8 ounces whole wheat pasta

Warm the oil in a large skillet over medium-high heat. When it's hot, add the garlic and onion and cook for 1 minute, or until fragrant. Add the bell pepper, mushrooms, and zucchini, and cook, stirring occasionally, for about 4 minutes, or until the vegetables are tender. Season with the salt and pepper to taste. Add the tomatoes, shrimp, oregano, basil, and thyme, and stir well to combine. Reduce the heat to low and simmer, partially covered, for about 7 minutes, or until the shrimp are pink.

Meanwhile, cook the pasta according to the package directions. Drain and place it in a large bowl.

Serve the pasta topped with the shrimp and vegetable mixture.

Makes 4 servings

Per serving: *388 calories, 34 g protein, 53 g carbohydrate, 6 g fat, 172 mg cholesterol, 467 mg sodium, 9 g fiber*

Diet Exchanges: *0 milk, 1½ vegetable, 0 fruit, 2½ bread, 3½ meat, 1 fat*

3½ Carb Choices

Elizabeth's Favorite Gumbo

—Elizabeth Martlock, Jim Thorpe, Pennsylvania

"For added flavor, roast Cajun seasoning in a pan until it's slightly darker in color, and add it to the soup. Serve hot, over rice or with bread. Enjoy!"

339 Calories

Prep time: 10 minutes
Cook time: 45 minutes

1½ pounds turkey sausage, preferably hot and spicy
½ cup vegetable oil
1 cup flour
2 tablespoons olive oil
3 boneless, skinless chicken breast halves, cut into thin strips
1 red bell pepper, finely chopped
1 green bell pepper, finely chopped
1 onion, finely chopped
3 cloves garlic, finely chopped
4 cans (28 ounces each) diced tomatoes
3 cups tomato juice
½ pound okra, sliced
¼ cup Cajun seasoning
2 cups small shrimp, shelled and deveined
Salt
Ground black pepper

Coat a large nonstick skillet with cooking spray and place it over medium-high heat. Add the sausage and cook for 10 minutes, or until brown. Remove from the heat, let cool, and cut into ½" slices. Set aside.

In a small skillet over medium heat, heat the vegetable oil. Add the flour and mix thoroughly with a wooden spoon. Cook for about 7 minutes, or until medium brown (almost milk chocolate) in color. Transfer to a heatproof container, and set aside.

In a large skillet over medium-high heat, heat the olive oil. Add the chicken and cook for 5 minutes, or until browned. Add the peppers and onion and cook for about 5 minutes, or until the vegetables begin to sweat. Add the garlic and cook for 1 minute.

Add the tomatoes, juice, okra, seasoning, shrimp, salt and pepper to taste, and sausage. Bring to a simmer. Slowly whisk in the reserved flour mixture. Cook for 10 minutes. Add the shrimp and cook for 5 minutes.

Makes 12 servings (24 cups)

Per serving: *339 calories, 24 g protein, 25 g carbohydrate, 17 g fat, 71 mg cholesterol, 1759 mg sodium, 1 g fiber*

Diet Exchanges: *0 milk, 2 vegetable, ½ fruit, ½ bread, 3 meat, 2½ fat*

2 Carb Choices

Pork Loin with Apple Cider Glaze

—Elizabeth Martlock, Jim Thorpe, Pennsylvania

402 Calories

"For a great accompaniment, serve with oven-roasted sweet potato wedges."

Prep time: 10 minutes
Marinate time: 4 hours
Cook time: 1 hour 15 minutes

- 1 small (1¾ pounds) pork loin
- 2 cloves garlic, finely chopped
  Salt
  Ground black pepper
- 3 cups apple cider
- 2 apples, chopped
- 1 bunch parsley, finely chopped (optional)

Rub the pork with garlic and salt and pepper to taste, and place it in an 8½" × 11" pan or a resealable plastic bag. Pour the apple cider around the pork, then add enough water to cover the pork. Let the pork marinate for 4 to 6 hours, or overnight.

Preheat oven to 350°F. Coat a 9" × 13" baking dish with cooking spray.

Place the pork in the prepared baking dish. Reserve the marinade. Bake for approximately 1 hour, or until a thermometer inserted in the center registers 150°F.

Meanwhile, in a saucepot, bring the marinade to a boil over high heat. Reduce the heat to medium-low and cook for about 20 minutes, or until the sauce is reduced by half to make a glaze. Add the apples and cook for 15 minutes.

Remove the pork from the oven and let it stand for 15 minutes before carving. Cut it into slices, and serve with the apple cider glaze. Sprinkle with the parsley, if using.

Makes 4 servings

Per serving: *402 calories, 41 g protein, 34 g carbohydrate, 11 g fat, 131 mg cholesterol, 116 mg sodium, 3 g fiber*

Diet Exchanges: *0 milk, 0 vegetable, 2 fruit, 0 bread, 6 meat, 0 fat*

2 Carb Choices

314 Calories

BBQ Pork Loin

—Anne Malone, Natick, Massachusetts

Prep time: 5 minutes
Marinate time: 1 hour
Bake time: 1 hour 35 minutes

- 3 tablespoons orange juice
- 1 cup chili sauce
- 2 cloves garlic, finely chopped
- 1 teaspoon onion salt
- 3½ pounds boneless pork loin

Preheat the oven to 350°F. Coat a baking dish with cooking spray.

In a large bowl or a resealable plastic bag, combine the juice, chili sauce, garlic, and onion salt. Add the pork and marinate for 1 hour. Remove the pork from the marinade, and place it in the baking dish. Bake for 1 hour 35 minutes, or until a thermometer inserted in the center registers 155°F.

Makes 8 servings

Per serving: *314 calories, 41 g protein, 11 g carbohydrate, 11 g fat, 131 mg cholesterol, 950 mg sodium, 0 g fiber*

Diet Exchanges: *0 milk, 0 vegetable, 0 fruit, 1 bread, 5 meat, 0 fat*

1 Carb Choice

SECRETS OF WEIGHT-LOSS WINNERS

• Clip out exercise tips and programs from *Prevention* magazine and other magazines, and put them in a binder. When you can't get to the gym, you'll have a variety of exercises that can be performed without equipment.

—Kelly Kennedy, Edmonton, Alberta, Canada

• Pull double-duty and turn reading time into exercise time, too, by picking up some books on tape or CD. Pop one in your portable player and hit the road for a walk that boosts your body and your brain power!

—*Prevention* magazine

304 Calories

Guava Pork Tenderloin

—Tyler McKinney, San Luis Obispo, California

"Guava nectar, available in larger grocery stores, lends a sweet-and-sour note to this flavorful pork dish."

Prep time: 5 minutes
Chill time: 3 hours
Cook time: 1 hour 45 minutes

1 can (12 ounces) guava nectar

2 teaspoons soy sauce

1 teaspoon cider vinegar

8 slices fresh gingerroot, each about ⅛" thick

½ teaspoon ground ginger

¼ cup packed brown sugar

4 pounds boneless center-cut pork loin

1 tablespoon olive oil

1 tablespoon cornstarch

¼ cup water

In a large resealable plastic bag, mix together the nectar, soy sauce, vinegar, gingerroot, ground ginger, and brown sugar. Add the pork, seal the bag, and refrigerate for at least 3 hours, or overnight.

Preheat the oven to 350°F.

Remove the pork from the marinade and wipe it dry with paper towels. Reserve the marinade.

Heat the oil in a large saucepan over high heat. Add the pork, and brown all sides.

Place the pork on a rack in a roasting pan and bake for 50 to 60 minutes, or until a thermometer inserted in the center registers 140°F. Remove the pork from the oven. Let it rest for 15 to 20 minutes before slicing.

While the pork is resting, in a small bowl, mix together the cornstarch and water. Set it aside. In a small saucepan over medium-high heat, bring the marinade to a boil. Reduce the heat to medium, add the cornstarch mixture, and cook for 3 minutes. Serve with the pork.

Makes 10 servings

Per serving: *304 calories, 37 g protein, 11 g carbohydrate, 11 g fat, 120 mg cholesterol, 180 mg sodium, 0 g fiber*

Diet Exchanges: *0 milk, 0 vegetable, ½ fruit, ½ bread, 4½ meat, ½ fat*

1 Carb Choice

307
Calories

Marinated Pork Chops
with Rosemary

—Melissa Dapkewicz, Fogelsville, Pennsylvania

Prep time: 5 minutes
Chill time: 1 hour
Cook time: 10 minutes

⅓ cup olive oil

⅓ cup dry red wine

3 tablespoons red wine vinegar

5 large cloves garlic, pressed

4 green onions, sliced

2 tablespoons chopped fresh rosemary,
+ additional sprigs for garnish

Salt

Ground black pepper

4 bone-in pork chops, each about 6 ounces

Whisk the oil, wine, vinegar, garlic, green onions, and rosemary together. Season to taste with salt and pepper. Put the pork chops in a glass baking dish and cover with the marinade. Refrigerate for 1 to 4 hours.

Coat a grill pan with cooking spray, and cook the chops for about 5 minutes per side, or until a thermometer inserted in the center registers 145°F. Garnish with sprigs of rosemary before serving.

Makes 4 servings

Per serving: *307 calories, 24 g protein, 3 g carbohydrate, 21 g fat, 61 mg cholesterol, 54 mg sodium, 1 g fiber*

Diet Exchanges: *0 milk, 0 vegetable, 0 fruit, 0 bread, 3 meat, 4 fat*

0 Carb Choice

545 Calories

Dorothy's Kugel

—Sandi Adler, Boca Raton, Florida

Prep time: 15 minutes
Cook time: 45 to 60 minutes

1 **package (1 pound) whole wheat egg noodles**
1 **container (16 ounces) low-fat sour cream**
1 **container (16 ounces) 1% cottage cheese**
1 **egg**
   Salt
   Ground black pepper
4 **tablespoons trans-free margarine**
¼ **cup fat-free milk**
⅓ **cup plain cornflake crumbs**

Preheat the oven to 350°F. Cook the noodles according to the package directions, and drain.

In a large bowl, combine the sour cream, cottage cheese, egg, and salt and pepper to taste. Add the noodles and stir to coat.

Coat a 9" × 13" microwaveable baking dish with cooking spray. Melt 1 tablespoon of the margarine in the dish in the microwave on medium for 30 seconds. Add the noodle mixture. Pour the milk around the edges, and sprinkle the top with the cornflake crumbs. Cut the remaining margarine into tablespoon-size slices, and sprinkle them onto the kugel. Bake for 45 to 60 minutes, or until browned on top.

Makes 8 servings

Per serving: *420 calories, 21 g protein, 52 g carbohydrate, 15 g fat, 50 mg cholesterol, 370 mg sodium, 3 g fiber*

Diet Exchanges: *0 milk, 0 vegetable, 0 fruit, 0 bread, 0 meat, 2 fat*

3½ Carb Choices

SHOPPING SAVVY
A Better Noodle

New on the shelves is Barilla's healthy pasta, Barilla Plus. It's multigrain, blending oats, spelt, and barley, plus legumes and flaxseed. Nutty-tasting and golden-colored, each 2-ounce serving provides 4 grams of fiber and 10 grams of protein. It's more assertive and firmer than all-white pasta, yet milder in flavor and not sticky, like some all-whole wheat pasta. Toss it with zesty marinara sauce, aromatic pesto, spicy red clam sauce, or garlic and olive oil. You could fool friends and neighbors with the

thin spaghetti or angel hair, which were kid-tested and approved by mom. Other shapes include penne, rotini, and elbows.

Easy Cheese Ravioli

283 Calories

—Thalia Gray, Scarborough, Ontario, Canada

"These ravioli can be prepared up to 2 hours ahead and refrigerated."

Prep time: 30 minutes
Cook time: 3 minutes

¾ **cup part-skim ricotta cheese**

¼ **cup grated, reduced-fat mozzarella cheese**

2 **tablespoons grated Parmesan cheese**

1 **egg**

¼ **cup chopped basil, + additional for garnish**

1 **clove garlic, finely chopped**

⅛ **teaspoon ground nutmeg**

1 **teaspoon salt**

Ground black pepper

24 **wonton wrappers**

2½ **cups tomato sauce**

In a medium bowl, combine the ricotta, mozzarella, Parmesan, egg, basil, garlic, nutmeg, and salt and pepper to taste. Place 1 rounded teaspoon of filling in the center of each wonton wrapper. Brush the edges of a wonton wrapper lightly with water. Fold the wrapper in half, making sure all the filling remains inside. Seal the edges by pinching. Continue with the remaining filling and wrappers.

Add salt to a large pot of boiling water. Gently add the ravioli, and cook for about 3 minutes, or until tender, stirring gently. Meanwhile, in a small pot over low heat, cook the tomato sauce. Using a large slotted spoon, place the ravioli into 4 individual bowls, pour the sauce over each serving, and garnish with the additional basil.

Makes 4 servings

Per serving: *283 calories, 15 g protein, 42 g carbohydrate, 7 g fat, 80 mg cholesterol, 1196 mg sodium, 3 g fiber*

Diet Exchanges: *0 milk, 2 vegetable, 0 fruit, 2 bread, 1 meat, 1 fat*

3 Carb Choices

Spinach Stuffed Shells

—Mary Conroy, Leechburg, Pennsylvania

306 Calories

Prep time: 10 minutes
Cook time: 25 minutes

12 jumbo pasta shells
 1 package (16 ounces) frozen chopped spinach, thawed and drained
 1 cup low-fat cottage cheese
 ½ cup mozzarella cheese, grated
 1 can (8 ounces) Italian spiced diced tomatoes, drained
   Salt
   Ground black pepper
 1 cup prepared pasta sauce
 ¼ cup grated Parmesan cheese

Preheat the oven to 375°F.

Cook the shells according to the package directions, and drain them well.

In a large mixing bowl, combine the spinach, cottage cheese, mozzarella, and tomatoes. Season to taste with salt and pepper.

Spread ¼ cup of the sauce on the bottom of an 8" × 11" baking dish. Stuff each shell with about ¼ cup of the spinach mixture, and arrange the shells in a single layer in the dish.

Pour the remaining sauce over the shells.

Cover with foil and bake for 15 to 20 minutes, or until the sauce is bubbling and the shells are heated through.

Sprinkle with the Parmesan cheese just before serving.

Makes 4 servings

Per serving: *306 calories, 22 g protein, 37 g carbohydrate, 8 g fat, 21 mg cholesterol, 729 mg sodium, 4 g fiber*

Diet Exchanges: *0 milk, 2½ vegetable, 0 fruit, 1½ bread, 2 meat, 1 fat*

2½ Carb Choices

Mushroom Strudel

—Theresa Wagner, Florida, New York

"This makes a wonderful lunch item along with a salad."

47 Calories

Prep time: 20 minutes
Cook time: 45 minutes

  8 ounces mushrooms, sliced

  1 small onion, chopped

2 or 3 cloves garlic, finely minced

  2 ounces low-fat cream cheese

  1 tablespoon chopped fresh chives

    Salt

    Ground black pepper

    A grating of fresh nutmeg

  6 sheets frozen 12" × 15" sheets phyllo dough, thawed

Preheat the oven to 375°F. Coat a baking sheet with cooking spray.

Lightly coat a large nonstick skillet with cooking spray and cook the mushrooms, onion, and garlic over high heat for about 10 minutes, or until the liquid has evaporated.

Stir in the cream cheese, chives, salt and pepper to taste, and nutmeg.

Lay the phyllo dough on a clean dish towel and spread the mushroom mixture about 1" away from the short edge of the dough. Fold the sides over about ½" and use the towel to help you roll it up like a jellyroll. Place the roll on the prepared baking sheet and coat it lightly with cooking spray.

Bake for 30 to 35 minutes, or until the phyllo is golden brown. Allow it to cool for 5 minutes before cutting individual portions.

Makes 12 servings

Per serving: *47 calories, 2 g protein, 7 g carbohydrate, 1 g fat, 3 mg cholesterol, 60 mg sodium, 1 g fiber*

Diet Exchanges: *0 milk, 0 vegetable, 0 fruit, ½ bread, 0 meat, 0 fat*

½ Carb Choice

Pasta with Chickpea Sauce

—Marvel Selke, Bandon, Oregon

456 Calories

"The sauce may be put in the blender if you prefer it less chunky."

Prep time: 10 minutes
Cook time: 23 minutes

1 tablespoon olive oil

1 onion, thinly sliced

4 cloves garlic, finely chopped

1 can (15 ounces) no-salt-added whole tomatoes

1 teaspoon dried whole rosemary, or 1 tablespoon fresh rosemary

2 cans (15 ounces each) chickpeas, drained and rinsed

½ pound whole wheat pasta

3 tablespoons finely chopped fresh parsley
  Ground black pepper

¼ cup Parmesan cheese (optional)

In a large saucepan, heat the oil over medium-high heat. Add the onion and cook for 3 minutes, or until soft. Add the garlic, and stir in the tomatoes and rosemary. Crush the tomatoes with the back of a wooden spoon. Add the chickpeas. Bring the mixture to a boil, then reduce the heat to low. Cook for 20 minutes, stirring occasionally.

Meanwhile, cook the pasta according to the package directions.

Sprinkle the sauce with the parsley and black pepper to taste, and spoon it over the pasta. Toss with the Parmesan cheese, if using.

Makes 4 servings

Per serving: *456 calories, 19 g protein, 78 g carbohydrate, 10 g fat, 0 mg cholesterol, 564 mg sodium, 16 g fiber*

Diet Exchanges: *0 milk, 1½ vegetable, 0 fruit, 4½ bread, 0 meat, 1½ fat*

5 Carb Choices

140 Calories

Tofu Stir-Fry

—Donna Johnson, Mount Vernon, Washington

Prep time: 10 minutes
Cook time: 10 minutes

2 tablespoons vegetable oil

1 red bell pepper, cut into ⅛" strips

¼ pound mushrooms, sliced

2 blocks (12 ounces each) 5-spice flavored firm tofu, drained and cubed

¼ bunch scallions, thinly sliced

1 teaspoon curry powder

Salt

Ground black pepper

1 tomato, finely chopped

1 tablespoon parsley, finely chopped

In a large saucepan, heat the oil over medium heat. Add the pepper and mushrooms, and cook for about 4 minutes, or until tender, stirring occasionally. Increase the heat to high and cook for 2 minutes, stirring until any liquid in the pan evaporates. Add the tofu, scallions, curry powder, and salt and pepper to taste. Reduce the heat to low, and cook for about 4 minutes, or until heated through. Stir in the tomato and parsley.

Makes 6 servings

Per serving: *140 calories, 11 g protein, 6 g carbohydrate, 10 g fat, 0 mg cholesterol, 16 mg sodium, 2 g fiber*

Diet Exchanges: *0 milk, 1 vegetable, 0 fruit, 0 bread, 1½ meat, 1 fat*

½ Carb Choice

Angel Hair Pasta with Fresh Tomato Sauce

—Janet Fricano, Fort Lee, New Jersey

467 Calories

"This recipe is delicious and satisfying; it helps me to lose weight and not feel hungry."

Prep time: 25 minutes
Stand time: 4 hours
Cook time: 10 minutes

10 medium tomatoes, chopped
 1 onion, chopped
 1 bunch fresh basil, thinly sliced, plus extra basil for garnish
 ¼ cup red wine vinegar
 2 tablespoons olive oil
 3 cloves garlic, minced
 1 teaspoon sugar
 1 package (1 pound) angel hair pasta
 8 ounces part-skim mozzarella cheese, grated

In a large bowl, combine the tomatoes, onion, basil, vinegar, oil, garlic, and sugar. Cover the bowl with plastic wrap and let it stand at room temperature for at least 4 hours.

When the sauce is ready, cook the pasta according to the package directions, and drain. Transfer the pasta to a large serving bowl, and cover with the sauce and cheese. Gently toss to mix well.

Makes 6 servings

Per serving: *467 calories, 21 g protein, 67 g carbohydrate, 15 g fat, 20 mg cholesterol, 276 mg sodium, 5 g fiber*

Diet Exchanges: *0 milk, 2 vegetable, 0 fruit, 3½ bread, 1½ meat, 2 fat*

4½ Carb Choices

YOU SAY TOMATO

We hope you say it often! Juicy, sweet tomatoes plucked fresh from the vine are one of summer's greatest pleasures. No matter how you slice them, these savory fruits add an irresistible tang to salads, sauces, salsas, and more. Don't avoid tomatoes in winter, either. When they're handled right and kept out of the fridge, they can provide plenty of juicy goodness.

Tomatoes are also packed with vitamin C, potassium, fiber, and lycopene, the pigment that colors tomatoes red—and fights disease. Traditionally, people have viewed lycopene as a "male nutrient" that protects against prostate cancer. But new evidence shows it can protect women's hearts, too. Lycopene may also play a role in stopping oral cancers related to smoking.

Lycopene is most concentrated in cooked tomato products. Some of the highest-yielding tomato products include a 6-ounce can of vegetable juice cocktail (17 mg), 1 cup of tomato soup (13 mg), and ¼ cup of marinara sauce (10 mg).

Here are a few quick ideas to get you thinking about new ways to eat tomatoes:

- Hollow out a tomato, reserving the insides. Make crab, tuna, egg, or chicken salad, mixing in the tomato pulp, and spoon it into the tomato shell.
- Layer ripe tomato slices with sliced avocado and red onion. Drizzle with fruity olive oil and sherry wine or balsamic vinegar.
- Arrange halved plum tomatoes on a baking sheet. Brush them lightly with olive oil, sprinkle with salt and pepper, and place a basil leaf on each. Roast at 325°F for about 45 minutes, or until they're softened and tender.
- Spread low-fat goat cheese on toasted whole grain bread. Top with tomato slices and grind fresh pepper over each. Or use smaller pieces of bread and chop the tomatoes to make bruschetta.

Potato Casserole

—Donna Rials, Lafayette, Louisiana

*"I like to substitute this dish for a baked potato with all the toppings.
You can serve it with salad and make it a meal, but it is a perfect
side dish for most meats and seafood!"*

219 Calories

Prep time: 15 minutes
Cook time: 40 minutes

6 Yukon Gold potatoes, cut into 1" cubes
½ cup reduced-sodium chicken broth
2 cloves garlic, minced
1 bunch scallions, sliced
½ cup mushrooms, sliced
½ teaspoon salt
¼ teaspoon ground black pepper
3 tablespoons soy-bacon bits
1 can (15 ounces) reduced-fat mushroom soup
⅓ cup shredded reduced-fat Cheddar cheese
1 cup Cheddar-fried onions

Preheat the oven to 350°F. Coat a 3-quart baking dish with cooking spray.

In a large saucepot fitted with a lid, boil the potatoes for about 20 minutes, or until they're tender. Drain and set them aside to cool briefly.

Meanwhile, heat the chicken broth in a large saucepan over medium heat. Add the garlic, scallions, mushrooms, salt, pepper, and bacon bits. Cook for about 5 minutes, or until the mushrooms are soft. Remove from the heat. Stir in the soup and the cheese.

Place the potatoes in the prepared baking dish.

Pour the sauce over the potatoes and top with the fried onions. Bake for 20 minutes, or until crispy on top.

Makes 8 servings

Per serving: *219 calories, 6 g protein, 30 g carbohydrate, 10 g fat, 7 mg cholesterol, 637 mg sodium, 3 g fiber*

Diet Exchanges: *0 milk, 1 vegetable, 0 fruit, 1½ bread, ½ meat, 1½ fat*

2 Carb Choices

177 Calories

Spinach Casserole

—Erin Monroe, Oviedo, Florida

"This casserole is great to keep on hand in the fridge for lunch. Its rich, cheesy flavor makes frozen pizzas and other fast food much less tempting."

Prep time: 10 minutes
Cook time: 1 hour

- 1 package (10 ounces) frozen chopped spinach, thawed and drained
- 1 container (15 ounces) part-skim ricotta cheese
- 6 ounces feta cheese, drained and crumbled
- 4 egg whites
- 1 teaspoon dried basil
- ½ teaspoon lemon pepper seasoning

Preheat the oven to 350°F. Coat a 9" × 13" baking dish with cooking spray.

In a large mixing bowl, combine the spinach, ricotta, feta, egg whites, basil, and lemon pepper. Pour the mixture into the prepared dish. Bake for 1 hour, or until the casserole is set and lightly browned around the edges.

Makes 6 servings

Per serving: *177 calories, 15 g protein, 7 g carbohydrate, 11 g fat, 54 mg cholesterol, 491 mg sodium, 1 g fiber*

Diet Exchanges: *0 milk, ½ vegetable, 0 fruit, 0 bread, 2 meat, 2 fat*

½ Carb Choice

Cabbage and Rice Casserole

—Irena Tatevosyan, Las Vegas, Nevada

"I love this dish because it contains many of my favorite ingredients. I usually eat it with baked fish drizzled with lemon juice."

223 Calories

Prep time: 20 minutes
Cook time: 35 minutes

    Salt
1 small head of cabbage, cut into
   8–10 pieces
1 cup quick-cooking brown rice
1 egg
2 cups low-fat sour cream
2 tablespoons unbleached or all-purpose
   flour
½ teaspoon baking soda
2 egg whites
¼ cup grated Parmesan cheese

Preheat the oven to 350°F. Coat an 8" × 8" baking dish with cooking spray.

Fill a large pot with water and salt to taste. Bring the water to a boil and add the cabbage. Boil the cabbage for 5 minutes. Drain and let chill in the refrigerator for at least 15 minutes.

Follow the package instructions to prepare the rice.

In a medium mixing bowl, combine the whole egg, sour cream, flour, and baking soda. Stir in the cooked rice. Arrange in a single layer in the bottom of the baking dish.

In a food processor, combine the cabbage and the egg whites. Pulse for 5 to 10 seconds, until the ingredients are thoroughly combined. Pour the cabbage mixture over the rice layer in the baking dish. Sprinkle the Parmesan cheese on top.

Bake for 35 to 40 minutes, or until lightly browned and puffy in the center.

Makes 6 servings

Per serving: *223 calories, 10 g protein, 25 g carbohydrate, 10 g fat, 65 mg cholesterol, 158 mg sodium, 3 g fiber*

Diet Exchanges: *0 milk, 1½ vegetable, 0 fruit, 1 bread, ½ meat, 2 fat*

2 Carb Choices

Creamed Spinach and Mushrooms

—Bobbi Campbell, San Antonio, Texas

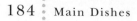
88 Calories

"It's surprisingly delicious and filling. I love to eat it, and it's healthy, but you'd never know it because it's so good."

Prep time: 13 minutes
Cook time: 14 minutes

½ tablespoon margarine
1 tablespoon canola oil
¼ pound mushrooms, sliced
3 cups spinach, stems removed, chopped
½ can (10¾ ounces) cream of mushroom soup
Salt
Ground black pepper

Heat the margarine and oil in a large saucepan over medium heat. Add the mushrooms, and cook for 7 minutes. Add the spinach, and cook for 3 minutes. Add the soup, and cook for about 4 more minutes. Season with the salt and pepper to taste.

Makes 4 servings

Per serving: *88 calories, 2 g protein, 4 g carbohydrate, 7 g fat, 0 mg cholesterol, 280 mg sodium, 1 g fiber*

Diet Exchanges: *0 milk, 1 vegetable, 0 fruit, 0 bread, 0 meat, 1½ fat*

½ Carb Choice

Breads, Breakfasts, Desserts, and Drinks

100 Calories

Light Beer Bread

—Jennifer Simonds, Vancouver, Washington

"Makes great toast or sandwich bread!"

Prep time: 6 minutes
Rise time: 15 minutes
Bake time: 1 hour

3 cups self-rising flour

2 tablespoons sugar

1 can (12 ounces) light beer, room temperature

1 egg, beaten with 1 tablespoon water

Preheat the oven to 375°F. Coat a nonstick bread pan with cooking spray.

In a large bowl, mix together the flour, sugar, and beer. Pour into the pan. Let the mixture sit for 15 minutes to rise, or until it has about doubled. Brush the top with the egg mixture and bake for about 1 hour.

Makes 16 servings

Per serving: *100 calories, 3 g protein, 19 g carbohydrate, 1 g fat, 13 mg cholesterol, 303 mg sodium, 1 g fiber*

Diet Exchanges: *0 milk, 0 vegetable, 0 fruit, 1½ bread, 0 meat, 0 fat*

1½ Carb Choices

Orange-Scented Scones with Craisins, Cherries, and Currants

215 Calories

—Elizabeth Martlock, Jim Thorpe, Pennsylvania

Prep time: 10 minutes
Bake time: 22 minutes

¾ **cup dried craisins**

¾ **cup dried currants**

¾ **cup dried cherries**

4½ **cups all-purpose flour, unbleached**

2 **tablespoons baking powder**

1 **teaspoon salt**

4 **tablespoons sugar**

2 **tablespoons vegetable oil**

1 **cup low-fat yogurt**

2 **teaspoons orange extract or**
  2 tablespoons orange zest

4 **egg whites, divided**

Preheat the oven to 400°F. Coat a baking dish with cooking spray.

In a small bowl, soak the craisins, currants, and cherries in warm water for about 5 minutes, or until they're softened and slightly plump. Drain them and discard the water.

In a large bowl, combine the flour, baking powder, salt, and 3 tablespoons of the sugar. Add the oil and use a pastry cutter or fork to evenly mix. Stir in the yogurt, orange extract or zest, and 3 of the egg whites. Then add the dried fruit, mixing just until it comes together. Place the dough onto a lightly coated surface, and knead just until thoroughly mixed. (Do not over-knead.)

Divide the dough into 2 balls. Flatten each into a disk about ¾" thick, then cut each disk into 8 wedges with a biscuit cutter. Place the wedges on the prepared baking sheet. Brush with the remaining egg white and sprinkle with the remaining sugar.

Bake for about 22 minutes, or until golden brown.

Makes 16 servings

Per serving: *215 calories, 6 g protein, 43 g carbohydrate, 2 g fat, 1 mg cholesterol, 321 mg sodium, 2 g fiber*

Diet Exchanges: *½ milk, 0 vegetable, 1 fruit, 1½ bread, 0 meat, 0 fat*

3 Carb Choices

169 Calories

Apricot Bran Muffins

—Marsha Galinksy, Pasadena, California

"Rather than reaching for an unhealthy snack when I crave something sweet, I reach for one of these healthy muffins, which completely satisfies my cravings. These muffins are high-fiber, low-fat, low-cholesterol, and very delicious!"

Prep time: 15 minutes
Bake time: 20 minutes

1⅓ cups unbleached or all-purpose flour
2 cups whole bran flakes cereal
½ teaspoon baking powder
½ teaspoon baking soda
¼ teaspoon salt
½ cup dried apricots, finely chopped
⅓ cup canola oil
½ cup light brown sugar
2 tablespoons molasses
¼ cup egg substitute
1 cup fat-free milk

Preheat the oven to 400°F. Coat a 12-cup nonstick muffin pan with cooking spray.

In a medium bowl, combine the flour, cereal, baking powder, baking soda, and salt. Fold in the apricots. In large bowl, combine the oil, sugar, molasses, and egg substitute, and beat until well combined. Add the flour mixture, then the milk, and stir with a fork until the dry ingredients are moistened. Do not beat.

Spoon the batter into the muffin tin and bake for 20 to 25 minutes, or until the muffins are golden and a wooden pick inserted in the center of a muffin comes out clean. Cool on a rack for 10 minutes before serving.

Makes 12 muffins

Per serving: *169 calories, 4 g protein, 26 g carbohydrate, 7 g fat, .5 mg cholesterol, 173 mg sodium, 4 g fiber*

Diet Exchanges: *0 milk, 0 vegetable, 0 fruit, 1½ bread, 0 meat, 1 fat*

½ Carb Choice

It Worked for Me!

Margaret Roach

VITAL STATS

Weight lost: 65 pounds

Time to goal: 1½ years

Greatest challenge: Being satisfied with her weight loss and trusting that she can maintain it

Growing up, Margaret Roach always had a sturdy, athletic figure. Her weight and shape were stable until, after her sons became young men, she took a position at a girls' boarding school. Living in a house of hearty eaters and working at a job that offered a buffet lunch every day made the extra pounds inevitable.

"I am originally from the South, and there is nothing more fattening than classic southern food. Up until about a year ago, for example, I would never have eaten chicken that wasn't fried. And I must mention that I'm lucky to have a husband who is down-to-earth and not concerned with appearances. But a breaking point came when I could not buy clothes that suited me; I had no choice but to buy whatever I could find in a big enough size. That was not acceptable, and I decided it was time to lose weight.

"I never could have done a typical weight-loss program. I would not be patient enough to count calories or disciplined enough to cut out certain foods completely. Instead, I ate what I always ate—and just cut my portions down to a third of my usual. I also learned to go more slowly by putting my fork down and engaging in conversation during meals.

"The staunch support of my coworker Kevin was crucial. I told him I was trying to lose weight and he would help me at lunchtime by "scoping out" the dining room and warning me if any of my favorites were being offered that day. If so, I would stick to the salad bar and not even wander near the buffet. Julie, Kevin's wife, was also a huge support, offering exercise advice and even planning out routines for me to do at home.

"Even with the extra weight, I always had excellent health—other than allergies requiring daily medicine. Now that I've lost the pounds, I notice that my respiratory problems are almost totally cleared up, I no longer get short of breath, and I rarely need allergy medication. Now I focus on accepting the new me and trusting that the world no longer sees me as a 'fat person.'"

www.eatupslimdown.com

High-Fiber Raisin Bran Muffins

122 Calories

—Andrea Hoorman, Columbus Grove, Ohio

"I love muffins but wanted them to be nutritious, low in calories and fat, and high in fiber. Since I changed to a high-fiber, low-fat diet after my second child, I lost 60 pounds and have kept it off for 1½ years now. These muffins are a great breakfast or anytime snack."

Prep time: 10 minutes
Bake time: 30 minutes

> 1 cup whole wheat pastry flour
> ¼ cup unbleached or all-purpose flour
> 2 teaspoons baking soda
> ¼ teaspoon salt
> ½ cup applesauce
> 1 teaspoon vanilla extract
> 1 egg + 1 egg white
> 1 apple, chopped
> ⅓ cup quick-cooking oats
> 1 teaspoon cinnamon
> ⅓ cup brown sugar
> 1 cup skim milk
> 2 cups raisin bran cereal

Preheat the oven to 350°F. Line a 12-cup muffin pan with paper muffin cups.

In a large mixing bowl, combine the flours, baking soda, and salt. Add the applesauce, vanilla, egg and egg white, apple, oats, cinnamon, and brown sugar. Stir well, and then add the cereal, stirring just until the mixture becomes moist. Spoon the mixture into each muffin cup, filling each cup about three-quarters full.

Bake for 30 to 35 minutes, or until a wooden pick inserted in the center of a muffin comes out clean. Cool on a rack for 10 minutes before serving.

Makes 12 muffins

Per serving: *122 calories, 4 g protein, 26 g carbo-hydrate, 1 g fat, 18 mg cholesterol, 221 mg sodium, 3 g fiber*

Diet Exchanges: *0 milk, 0 vegetable, 0 fruit, 1½ bread, 0 meat, 0 fat*

1½ Carb Choices

Lighten-Up Blueberry Muffins

121 Calories

—Deborah Shealy, Lexington, South Carolina

"I love blueberry muffins, but even the low-fat versions in the store are high in calories. This recipe lowers both the fat and calories. I often eat one for breakfast with a cup of yogurt or later in the day as a midafternoon snack."

Prep time: 10 minutes
Bake time: 20 minutes

1¾ **cups whole grain pastry flour**
2½ **teaspoons baking powder**
½ **teaspoon cinnamon**
½ **teaspoon salt**
¾ **cup trans-free margarine or butter**
½ **cup Splenda**
½ **cup + 1 tablespoon sugar**
¾ **cup 1% milk**
1 **egg**
1 **cup fresh blueberries**

Preheat the oven to 375°F. Lightly coat an 18-cup muffin pan with cooking spray.

In a small bowl, sift together the flour, baking powder, cinnamon, and salt.

In a large bowl, combine the margarine or butter, Splenda, and ½ cup of the sugar. Beat with an electric mixer on medium speed for 2 minutes, or until fluffy. Add the milk and egg. Beat for another minute (the mixture will look separated). Add the butter mixture and stir just until combined. In the same small bowl, toss the blueberries with the remaining tablespoon of sugar and fold them gently into the batter.

Spoon the mixture into each muffin cup, filling each cup two-thirds full.

Bake for 20 minutes, or until the muffins are slightly browned and a wooden pick inserted in the center of a muffin comes out clean. Cool on a rack for 10 minutes before serving.

Makes 18 muffins

Per serving: *121 calories, 2 g protein, 16 g carbohydrate, 6 g fat, 22 mg cholesterol, 192 mg sodium, 1 g fiber*

Diet Exchanges: *0 milk, 0 vegetable, 0 fruit, 1 bread, 0 meat, 1 fat*

1 Carb Choice

BLUEBERRIES: THE WONDER FRUIT

Luscious, naturally sweet blueberries are jam-packed with health benefits. With only 80 calories and 3.9 grams of fiber per cup, they are a good source of vitamin C, and they're an excellent way to get more fiber.

Enjoy half a cup a day of these fabulous berries, nature's number-one source of antioxidants. The antioxidants in blueberries may help to halt the forces that cause aging. Much of this power comes, literally "out of the blue" from anthocyanins, the pigments that give the berries their deep blue hue. Blueberries are bursting with them. Even the scientists who study blueberries are excited—and are making blueberries a part of their own daily diets.

There is also a possibility that blueberries can actually reverse the loss of short-term memory that happens as we age, according to USDA scientist James Joseph, PhD. Research is also planned to examine the ability of blueberries to prevent macular degeneration, a common eye disease that many people experience with aging.

The blueberry is native to North America. Found fresh in stores nearly year-round, most are grown by producers across the United States and Canada. In November and December, look for some large and noteworthy berries (about the size of a quarter) imported from New Zealand.

But the domestic, seasonal, highbush blueberries are what most of us treasure and are willing to wait for. Their season is short, from mid-June to mid-August, so when they appear in stores, fresh and firm, with a silvery bloom—and at a good price—buy plenty and freeze the extras.

To successfully freeze blueberries, don't wash them, and make sure they are completely dry. You can overwrap the store container with a zip-top freezer bag and label and date it, or you can transfer the berries in measured amounts into freezer bags. Write the cup amount on the bag—never believe that you might remember how much is in there when you decide you want to use them!

Once frozen, blueberries will keep for a year or so. Use them while still frozen, unless a recipe tells you to do otherwise.

11 WAYS TO TURN BLUE

Blueberries are really the no-work fruit—there's no pitting, peeling, coring, or cutting. A quick rinse and they're ready to roll. Try these quick ideas for getting the anti-aging power of the blues every day.

Breakfast cereal boost. Sprinkle ½ cup or more of blueberries on your favorite cereal. If you use frozen berries, let them sit for about 5 minutes first.

Blueberry-yum pancakes. Make up your favorite whole grain pancake batter. Fold in fresh berries or scatter frozen berries onto the pools of batter just after they've been dropped onto the griddle. (That way, the berries will stay juicier and won't sink.)

Blue-ricotta spread. Mix coarsely chopped blueberries into part-skim ricotta cheese. Spread it on toasted pumpernickel bread and sprinkle with cinnamon for breakfast or a snack.

Red, white, and blue salad. On a bed of mixed greens, sprinkle low-fat feta cheese, sliced strawberries, and blueberries. Toss with vinaigrette dressing.

Fruit salad super-combos. Arrange avocado slices, cantaloupe cubes, and blueberries; drizzle with honey vinaigrette. Or mix watermelon cubes, kiwifruit slices, and blueberries—delicious as is.

Dessert cooler. Pair blueberries with lemon, raspberry, or melon sorbet. Decorate with a mint sprig and lemon twist.

Fruity yogurt. Stir up half low-fat vanilla or lemon yogurt and half fresh or frozen blueberries. More berries means less sugar—and terrific flavor.

Ginger-peachy blues. Chop peaches into chunks, and shower them with blueberries and chopped crystallized ginger.

Blue and smooth. Blend frozen blueberries, a banana, skim milk, a pinch of cinnamon, and crushed ice for a wild smoothie.

Quick blueberry pandowdy. In a glass baking dish, mix 3 cups of blueberries, ½ cup of purple grape juice, ½ tablespoon of cornstarch, and 3 low-fat cereal bars, crumbled. Cover and microwave on high for 7 to 10 minutes, or until bubbly. Stir and serve hot (serves 4).

Blueberry jimmies. Kids love this one: Fill an ice cream cone with low-fat vanilla ice cream or frozen yogurt. Allow the outer surface of the ice cream or yogurt to soften a bit, then roll it in fresh or frozen (slightly thawed) blueberries. Wild blueberries, because they are smaller, work best.

Dawn's "Oh-So-Filling" Muffins

—Dawn Stickney, Tyngsboro, Massachusetts

117 Calories

"At about 3 o'clock in the afternoon, I am always looking for something sweet to eat. By adding the brown sugar to the tops of these muffins, I got that sweetness I was looking for and the high fiber and protein to fill me up until dinnertime."

Prep time: 10 minutes
Bake time: 18 minutes

 1 cup whole wheat flour
½ cup whole oats
¼ cup ground flax seeds
 2 teaspoons baking powder
½ cup sugar
¾ cup rice milk
¼ cup canola oil
 1 egg
 1 cup chopped cranberries
¼ cup walnuts, coarsely chopped
¼ cup brown sugar (optional)

Preheat the oven to 350°F. Line a muffin pan with paper baking cups.

In a mixing bowl, combine the flour, oats, flax seeds, baking powder, and sugar. Add the milk, oil, and egg. Mix thoroughly until well combined. Fold in the cranberries and nuts. Spoon the mixture into each muffin cup, filling each cup two-thirds full. Sprinkle the brown sugar on the muffin tops, if using. Bake for 15 to 18 minutes, or until golden brown.

Makes 18 muffins

Per serving: *117 calories, 3 g protein, 15 g carbohydrate, 6 g fat, 12 mg cholesterol, 51 mg sodium, 2 g fiber*

Diet Exchanges: *0 milk, 0 vegetable, 0 fruit, 1 bread, 0 meat, 1 fat*

1 Carb Choice

Pumpkin Gingerbread Loaf

—Tina Foster, Cobble Hill, British Columbia, Canada

"All of my loaves and muffins are egg, butter, and oil free. Really, it's easy to take these ingredients out of any muffin recipe—just use low-fat milk, applesauce, or other pureed fruit to replace the moisture."

158 Calories

Prep time: 15 minutes
Bake time: 40 minutes

- 2 cups whole grain pastry flour
- 1½ teaspoons ground ginger
- 1 teaspoon baking soda
- ½ teaspoon salt
- 1½ teaspoons cinnamon
- ½ teaspoon ground cloves
- ½ cup molasses
- ¾ cup light soy milk
- 1 tablespoon grated fresh ginger (optional)
- 1 cup pumpkin puree
- ½ cup walnuts, chopped

Preheat the oven to 350°F. Coat a nonstick bread pan with cooking spray.

In a large bowl, combine the flour, ginger, baking soda, salt, cinnamon, and cloves. In a separate large bowl, mix together the molasses and milk. Add the flour mixture and the fresh ginger, if using. Add the pumpkin and the walnuts. Pour the batter into the prepared pan. Bake for 40 to 45 minutes, or until a wooden pick inserted in the center comes out clean. Let the bread cool before slicing.

Makes 1 loaf (12 slices)

Per serving: *158 calories, 3 g protein, 29 g carbohydrate, 4 g fat, 0 mg cholesterol, 243 mg sodium, 3 g fiber*

Diet Exchanges: *0 milk, 0 vegetable, 0 fruit, 2 bread, 0 meat, ½ fat*

2 Carb Choices

Southwestern Frittata

—Margaret Stephens, Oklahoma City, Oklahoma

Prep time: 10 minutes
Cook time: 20 minutes

  1 tablespoon olive oil
  1 green bell pepper, diced
  1 sweet onion, diced
  4 Roma tomatoes, diced
  4 eggs, lightly beaten
    Salt
    Ground black pepper

Preheat the oven to 350°F.

In a medium, oven-safe, nonstick skillet, heat the oil over medium heat. Add the pepper and onion, and cook for 5 minutes, or until the onion is translucent. Add the tomatoes and eggs. Stir constantly until the egg is distributed all over the bottom of the pan. Cook for 1 or 2 minutes, or until the eggs begin to set. Season with salt and pepper to taste.

Bake in the oven for 10 minutes, or until the eggs are cooked and the mixture has puffed slightly. Let the frittata cool slightly and cut it into wedges for serving.

Makes 4 servings

Per serving: *81 calories, 5 g protein, 8 g carbohydrate, 4 g fat, 0 mg cholesterol, 60 mg sodium, 2 g fiber*

Diet Exchanges: *0 milk, 1½ vegetable, 0 fruit, 0 bread, ½ meat, ½ fat*

1½ Carb Choices

Scrambled Egg Wrap

—Julie Johnson, Niagara Falls, Ontario, Canada

274 Calories

"It's a great way to start your morning; it's light but not too filling. It makes you want to eat in the morning instead of skipping breakfast, because it's fast and easy to prepare."

Prep time: 5 minutes
Cook time: 5 minutes

2 **eggs, lightly beaten**
2 **tablespoons herb cream cheese spread**
1 **whole wheat soft taco wrap**
2 **tablespoons low-fat grated cheddar cheese**
½ **tablespoon chopped fresh basil**
½ **tablespoon chopped fresh chives**
1 **tablespoon salsa**

Preheat the oven to warm. Coat a small skillet with cooking spray. Add the eggs to the skillet and cook for 2 minutes, stirring constantly. Spread the cheese spread on the wrap, then add the eggs, cheese, basil, chives, and salsa. Roll up the wrap, folding in the sides, and heat it in the oven for 3 minutes, or until warmed through.

Makes 1 serving

Per serving: *274 calories, 20 g protein, 22 g carbohydrate, 14 g fat, 436 mg cholesterol, 504 mg sodium, 2 g fiber*

Diet Exchanges: *0 milk, 1 vegetable, 0 fruit, 1 bread, 2½ meat, 2 fat*

1½ Carb Choices

SHOPPING SAVVY
Eggs-cellent

If you're watching fat and cholesterol but love eggs, check out Eggology refrigerated 100 percent fresh egg whites. Use for scrambles, omelets, casseroles, and French toast, and never deal with that "extra" egg yolk again. Unsure about an all-white omelet? Jazz it up with chopped parsley or tomato. Or use it to replace whole eggs for most baking, and for meringues and frosting. Super-fresh, the whites are "cracked and packed within 3 days of leaving the ranch," says chief Eggsecutive Brad Halpern.

Pasteurized, tested for salmonella and listeria, and available as organic. Available in 32- and 16-ounce containers, or 4-packs of microwaveable 4 ounce single-serving cups. Look for it at supermarkets and natural food stores nationwide.

Bacon, Mushroom, and Pepper Scramble

—Jennifer Chadwell, Arlington, Texas

172 Calories

"I am a firm believer that eggs are a great source of protein without the bad fats. This filling dish is perfect served with whole grain rye toast, and it can be enjoyed any time of day."

Prep time: 10 minutes
Cook time: 13 minutes

3 slices turkey bacon
½ onion, finely chopped
¼ cup finely chopped green bell pepper
1 cup sliced mushrooms
6 eggs
1 teaspoon Cajun seasoning
   Salt
   Ground black pepper
¼ cup grated Parmesan cheese

In a medium, nonstick skillet over medium heat, cook the bacon for about 5 minutes, or until it's brown and crisp. Transfer the bacon to a plate lined with paper towels.

Add the onion, bell pepper, and mushrooms to the skillet. Reduce the heat slightly and cook for about 5 minutes, or until the vegetables are softened, stirring occasionally.

Meanwhile, whisk the eggs in a small bowl. Add the Cajun seasoning, and salt and pepper to taste. Pour the eggs into the pan and scramble for 3 to 5 minutes, or until set. Just before removing the eggs from the skillet, crumble the bacon over the eggs and sprinkle with the cheese.

Makes 4 servings

Per serving: *172 calories, 14 g protein, 4 g carbohydrate, 11 g fat, 331 mg cholesterol, 445 mg sodium, 1 g fiber*

Diet Exchanges: *0 milk, ½ vegetable, 0 fruit, 0 bread, 2 meat, 1½ fat*

1½ Carb Choices

It Worked for Me!

Trudy Rogers-Moore

VITAL STATS

Weight lost: 40 pounds

Time to goal: 2 years and holding

Greatest challenge: Preventing exercise "burn-out"

A car accident led to chronic back pain for Trudy Rogers-Moore. This formerly active woman—a runner and ball player—found herself forced to the sidelines and gaining weight. Trudy sought out a new, back-friendly way to move and burn calories, and she's stuck with it ever since.

"In March of 2001, a car accident changed my life. I sustained a lower-back injury that prevented me from taking part in any strenuous physical activity. It was only a matter of time before the pounds started to stick. The first thing I did was change my diet to include more whole grains and salads, and I began to drink much more water, but I was still missing the exercise component.

"I was up late one night, actually nursing a backache, when I saw a television commercial for a low-impact exercise machine called 'the Gazelle.' Tony Little, the device's inventor, told an inspiring story of having been in many accidents himself—and there was a money-back guarantee—so I picked up the phone at 2 A.M. and ordered it. It arrived within a week and my husband put it together for me.

"I have never regretted that impulse purchase. In fact, I tell people now that I would be a spokesperson for the Gazelle if I could! I use it for 45 minutes every weekday morning, and do a lot of walking during the weekends. The Gazelle's gliding, almost effortless movement does not hurt my back at all. The machine is totally human-powered and the smooth action is similar to cross-country skiing. I find it is a great stress reliever for me, and I've never felt this good.

"At the beginning, I was so excited to be active again and so eager to lose the extra weight that I would push myself to work out more than once a day. I realized, though, that I could wind up becoming bored or even getting injured, so I had to stop myself. Now I take it day by day, and I am very happy with my renewed ability to exercise, the pounds I've lost, and the muscle I've gained."

147 Calories

Light Oatmeal Cake

—Nancy Russeau, Maybee, Michigan

"We all know that oatmeal is good for the heart, but this dessert has few calories, too! Eating small pieces helped me lose weight because I was able to avoid other desserts that had more sugar."

Prep time: 15 minutes
Bake time: 30 minutes

2 cups boiling water
1 cup rolled oats
½ cup trans-free margarine
⅓ cup brown sugar
1 cup Splenda Sugar Blend for Baking
2 large eggs
1 teaspoon vanilla extract
1½ cups all-purpose flour
1 teaspoon baking soda
2 teaspoons ground cinnamon
1 teaspoon ground nutmeg
½ teaspoon salt
1 tablespoon confectioners' sugar

Preheat the oven to 350°F. Coat a 9" × 13" cake pan with nonstick cooking spray.

In a small bowl, combine the water with the oats, and set aside.

In large bowl, use an electric mixer to cream together the margarine, brown sugar, Splenda, eggs, and vanilla for about 1 minute, or until smooth. Add the oats. Fold in the flour, baking soda, cinnamon, nutmeg, and salt. Mix until well combined.

Pour the batter into the prepared pan and bake for 30 minutes, or until a wooden pick inserted in the center of the cake comes out clean. Cool on a wire rack and dust with the confectioners' sugar just before serving.

Makes 16 servings

Per serving: *147 calories, 3 g protein, 18 g carbohydrate, 7 g fat, 26 mg cholesterol, 224 mg sodium, 1 g fiber*

Diet Exchanges: *0 milk, 0 vegetable, 0 fruit, 1 bread, 0 meat, 1 fat*

1 Carb Choice

Sally's Healthy Bread Pudding

— Sally Waggoner, Muncie, Indiana

211 Calories

"This sweet dessert isn't as rich as the version my mother used to make with heavy cream, but the fact that it's so much healthier makes it taste just as delicious."

Prep time: 8 minutes
Bake time: 40 minutes

6 slices whole grain bread, cut into ½" cubes

1 cup fat-free half-and-half

2 tablespoons butter

1 tablespoon flour

2 cups skim milk

1 cup fresh or frozen blueberries

¼ cup orange juice

3 large eggs, beaten

2 egg whites, lightly beaten

2 tablespoons brown sugar

1 teaspoon vanilla extract

¼ teaspoon ground allspice

Preheat the oven to 350°F. Coat a 6-cup baking dish with cooking spray. Place the bread in the baking dish. Set aside.

In a large saucepan, melt the butter and stir in the flour. Blend well and cook over low heat. Do not brown. Add the milk, stirring constantly for about 5 minutes, or until the mixture thickens.

In a small bowl, combine the spread, orange juice, egg, egg whites, sugar, rum, and allspice.

Add to the saucepan, stirring until well mixed. Pour the mixture over the bread cubes and stir just until coated.

Bake uncovered for 40 minutes, or until the top is golden and the pudding is firm to the touch.

Makes 6 servings

Per serving: *211 calories, 10 g protein, 34 g carbohydrate, 4 g fat, 107 mg cholesterol, 236 mg sodium, 2 g fiber*

Diet Exchanges: *½ milk, 0 vegetable, ½ fruit, 1 bread, ½ meat, ½ fat*

2 Carb Choices

Cranberry-Apple Crumble

—Patricia Antoine, Dorchester, Massachusetts

"Last year during the holidays I was pregnant and I knew I would overdo it with desserts and regret it, since I have unstable blood sugar. So I came up with this little sweet-tooth satisfier and had requests from both my parents and my siblings to make it again!"

181 Calories

Prep time: 10 minutes
Bake time: 30 minutes

FILLING

- 4 medium apples, cored and coarsely chopped
- 2 cups whole fresh cranberries
- ¼ cup instant granulated tapioca pearls
- ¼ cup warm water
- 1 teaspoon cinnamon
- ½ teaspoon nutmeg
- ½ teaspoon cloves
- ½ cup sugar

TOPPING

- ⅓ cup sliced almonds
- 2 tablespoons brown sugar
- 2 tablespoons flour
- 2 tablespoons nonhydrogenated vegetable spread

Preheat the oven to 350°F. Lightly coat a glass pie plate with cooking spray.

To make the filling: In a large bowl, combine the apples, cranberries, tapioca, water, cinnamon, nutmeg, cloves, and sugar. Let stand for 10 minutes.

Pour the fruit into the prepared glass pie plate.

To make the topping: In a small bowl, combine the almonds, brown sugar, flour, and vegetable spread until crumbly. Sprinkle on top of the fruit.

Bake for 35 to 40 minutes, or until the top is golden brown and the juice is mostly absorbed.

Makes 8 servings

Per serving: *181 calories, 2 g protein, 36 g carbohydrate, 4 g fat, 0 mg cholesterol, 30 mg sodium, 5 g fiber*

Diet Exchanges: *0 milk, 0 vegetable, 1 fruit, 1½ bread, 0 meat, ½ fat*

2½ Carb Choices

191 Calories

Greek Peach
—Pat Martin, Chicago, Illinois

"For everyone who likes the smell of peach cobbler and the thick, gooey filling, this pastry has all the sensual ingredients, plus everyone feels light leaving the table."

Prep time: 15 minutes
Bake time: 8 minutes

1 teaspoon cornstarch
1½ teaspoons cold water
3 cups sliced peaches, fresh or frozen
½ teaspoon cinnamon
¼ teaspoon nutmeg
⅛ teaspoon mace
½ teaspoon allspice
3 teaspoons Splenda
2 tablespoons honey
3 tablespoons margarine
1 vanilla bean, soaked, split in half
1 package phyllo dough
¾ cup frozen vanilla yogurt (optional)

Preheat the oven to 375°F. Coat a muffin pan with cooking spray.

In a small bowl, whisk together the cornstarch and water.

In a medium saucepot over medium-high heat, combine the peaches, cinnamon, nutmeg, mace, allspice, sugar substitute, and honey. Add the cornstarch mixture to the peaches and cook for about 2 minutes, or until the sauce thickens and the peaches are tender.

Melt the margarine in a large skillet. Scrape out the seeds from the vanilla bean and add them to the margarine.

Brush 1 sheet of the phyllo with melted margarine. Add a second sheet of phyllo on top, and brush with margarine. Cut into 12 equal squares. Place each square in a muffin tin and press to form the muffin tin shape. Bake for 8 minutes, or until golden. Cool.

Once the peach mixture and phyllo dough cups have cooled, scoop the peaches into the cups. Just before serving, top each phyllo cup with 1 tablespoon of frozen yogurt, if using.

Makes 6 servings

Per serving: *191 calories, 3 g protein, 31 g carbohydrate, 7 g fat, 0 mg cholesterol, 184 mg sodium, 3 g fiber*

Diet Exchanges: *0 milk, 0 vegetable, 1 fruit, 1 bread, 0 meat, 1 fat*

2 Carb Choices

Creamy Applesauce Dream

—Amy Tucker, Vancouver, British Columbia, Canada

"This dish, which tastes great warm or cold, has helped me keep on track whenever I am craving something like apple pie and ice cream. It's much more satisfying than any other treat."

Prep time: 15 minutes
Cook time: 30 minutes

  3 **pounds apples (9 or 10 medium apples), peeled, cored, and quartered**
  ¼ **cup orange juice**
  2 **teaspoons vanilla extract**
  2 **teaspoons cinnamon**
  ¼ **cup low-fat, sugar-free frozen yogurt (optional)**

In a large saucepot, combine the apples, orange juice, vanilla, and cinnamon. Cover and simmer for 30 minutes, or until the apples are tender, stirring occasionally. Mash the apples with a potato ricer until smooth. Top each serving with 1½ teaspoons yogurt, if using.

Makes 8 servings, ½ cup each

Per serving: *96 calories, 0 g protein, 26 g carbohydrate, 0 g fat, 0 mg cholesterol, 0 mg sodium, 6 g fiber*

Diet Exchanges: *0 milk, 0 vegetable, 1½ fruit, 0 bread, 0 meat, 0 fat*

1½ Carb Choices

Pumpkin Custard

—Shirley Hill, Chatham, Ontario, Canada

205 Calories

"This pumpkin custard allows me to enjoy a healthy, appetizing dessert and provides extra fiber and calcium. While eating it, I've been able to maintain a steady, 1-pound-a-week weight loss. Hurray for pumpkin custard!"

Prep time: 5 minutes
Cook time: 7 minutes

½ cup sugar

2 large eggs

1 cup (12 ounces) fat-free, evaporated skim milk

1 cup cold water

1 can (16 ounces) pumpkin puree

½ teaspoon ground nutmeg

1 teaspoon vanilla extract

In a large microwaveable bowl, blend together the sugar and eggs. Add the milk, water, pumpkin, nutmeg, and vanilla. Microwave on high for 3 minutes. Stir, then return the mixture to the microwave for another 3 to 4 minutes, or until the mixture thickens. Divide into 6 individual serving bowls.

Makes 6 servings

Per serving: *205 calories, 6 g protein, 40 g carbohydrate, 2 g fat, 72 mg cholesterol, 175 mg sodium, 2 g fiber*

Diet Exchanges: *½ milk, 0 vegetable, 0 fruit, 2 bread, ½ meat, 0 fat*

2½ **Carb Choices**

Carrot Pineapple Gelatin

—Lisa Zucknick, Taylor, Texas

104 Calories

"This refreshing dessert is simple to make and satisfies my sweet tooth well. It can also be served as a side dish."

Prep time: 5 minutes
Chill time: 1 hour 10 minutes

1 package (3 ounces) orange flavored gelatin
1 small can (15 ounces) crushed pineapple, drained
1 cup shredded carrots

In a large glass bowl, prepare the gelatin according to the package directions. Put in the refrigerator for about 40 minutes, to chill slightly. Then add the pineapple and carrots and chill for about 30 minutes, or until firm.

Makes 6 servings

Per serving: *104 calories, 6 g protein, 21 g carbohydrate, 1 g fat, 0 mg cholesterol, 37 mg sodium, 1 g fiber*

Diet Exchanges: *0 milk, 0 vegetable, 1 fruit, ½ bread, ½ meat, 0 fat*

1½ Carb Choices

Peachy Frozen Yogurt

—Janet Fricano, Fort Lee, New Jersey

"This luscious frozen dessert is a healthy alternative to ice cream."

144 Calories

Prep time: 8 minutes
Freeze time: 10 hours

> 3 **cups frozen peaches or nectarines, partially thawed**
>
> 2 **cartons (16 ounces each) low-fat vanilla yogurt**
>
> ¼ **cup honey**

Place 1½ cups of the peaches in a food processor with the yogurt and honey. Process until smooth. Finely chop the remaining peaches and stir into the yogurt mixture. Pour into a 2-quart pan. Cover and freeze for 4 hours, or until firm.

Break the frozen mixture into small pieces and place in the food processor. Pulse until fluffy. Return the mixture to the pan and freeze, covered, for 6 hours or until firm.

Let the frozen yogurt stand at room temperature for 15 minutes before serving.

Makes 12 servings, ½ cup each

Per serving: *144 calories, 4 g protein, 31 g carbohydrate, 1 g fat, 4 mg cholesterol, 54 mg sodium, 1 g fiber*

Diet Exchanges: *0 milk, 0 vegetable, 2 fruit, 0 bread, 0 meat, 0 fat*

2 Carb Choices

SHOPPING SAVVY
Luscious and Light

Breyers has a new premium ice cream, Breyers Light. It tastes scrumptious, and it won't blow your diet. Made with all-natural ingredients in everyone's favorite flavors: Creamy Vanilla; Vanilla Bean; Creamy Chocolate; a Vanilla, Chocolate, and Strawberry trio; Mint Chocolate Chip;

Butter Pecan; and even Rocky Road. A ½-cup serving ranges from 100 to 140 calories and from 3.5 to 5 grams of fat—half the fat and 25 percent fewer calories than regular ice cream. Breyers Light is found in 56-ounce containers in grocery freezers nationwide.

203 Calories

Chocolate Tofu Pudding

—Sherrion Pennington, Wenatchee, Washington

"This healthy pudding makes me feel like I've had a delicious desert, without the calories."

Prep time: 8 minutes

- 1 package (14 ounces) light firm silken tofu, drained
- ¾ cup skim milk
- ¾ cup semisweet chocolate chips, melted
- 1 container (8 ounces) frozen fat-free whipped topping, thawed
- ¼ cup grated dark chocolate (for garnish)

In a food processor, pulse the tofu for 10 to 15 seconds, or until smooth. Gradually add the milk and beat until smooth.

Add the melted chocolate. Pulse for about 1 minute, or until smooth. Remove the mixture to a bowl and fold in the whipped topping. Garnish with dark chocolate, if using.

Makes 8 servings, ½ cup each

Per serving: *203 calories, 6 g protein, 23 g carbohydrate, 9 g fat, .5 mg cholesterol, 65 mg sodium, 2 g fiber*

Diet Exchanges: *0 milk, 0 vegetable, 0 fruit, 1½ bread, ½ meat, 1 fat*

1½ Carb Choices

197 Calories

Raspberry Heaven

—Nancy Nelson, Farmington, New Mexico

"When I need to feel I'm having something decadently and sinfully sweet, this recipe does the trick while still keeping me on track with my diet."

Prep time: 5 minutes
Chill time: 12 hours

1 container (8 ounces) fat-free whipped topping, thawed

1 container (16 ounces) low-fat cottage cheese

1 package (3 ounces) sugar-free raspberry-flavored gelatin

1 package (12 ounces) frozen unsweetened raspberries, thawed

In a large bowl, mix together the whipped topping and cottage cheese. Fold in the gelatin until thoroughly combined. Add the raspberries.

Refrigerate, covered, for 12 hours before serving.

Makes 6 servings

Per serving: *197 calories, 16 g protein, 20 g carbohydrate, 1 g fat, 3 mg cholesterol, 342 mg sodium, 1 g fiber*

Diet Exchanges: *0 milk, 0 vegetable, ½ fruit, 1 bread, 1 meat, 0 fat*

1½ Carb Choices

Iced Lemons with Raspberries and Mint

—Elizabeth Martlock, Jim Thorpe, Pennsylvania

172 Calories

Prep time: 25 minutes
Cook time: 3 minutes
Chill time: At least 7 hours

  8 **lemons**
  ½ **cup water**
  4 **mint leaves**
1½ **cups sugar**
1½ **cups frozen raspberries**

Slice the tops off of the lemons to make toppers. Scoop out the insides of the lemons and strain to create 1 cup of juice. Discard the pulp and reserve the excess juice for future use.

Place the empty lemon shells and toppers on a baking sheet and place them in the freezer until the filling is ready.

Bring the water, mint, and sugar to a boil in a small saucepan over low heat. Boil for 2 to 3 minutes, or until the sugar has dissolved. Remove from the heat, strain, and set aside to cool. Remove and discard the mint leaves.

Add the lemon juice to the cooled syrup mixture. Freeze the syrup mixture for at least 4 hours, or overnight.

When the mixture is frozen, place it in a food processor and process until creamy. Fold in the raspberries and freeze for at least 3 hours.

To assemble the dessert, pack the lemon-raspberry filling into the frozen lemon shells, place the toppers on, and return to the freezer until needed.

Makes 8 servings

Per serving: *172 calories, 1 g protein, 44 g carbohydrate, 0 g fat, 0 mg cholesterol, 1 mg sodium, 1 g fiber*

Diet Exchanges: *0 milk, 0 vegetable, ½ fruit, 2 bread, 0 meat, 0 fat*

3 Carb Choices

Mandarin Delight

—Susan Johnson, Guntersville, Alabama

320 Calories

"This is a wonderful, low-fat way to satisfy a sweet tooth!"

Prep time: 5 minutes
Chill time: 2 hours

- 1 package (3 ounces) orange-flavored sugar-free gelatin
- 1 cup fat-free cottage cheese
- 1 container (8 ounces) fat-free whipped topping
- 1 cup miniature marshmallows
- 2 cans (11 ounces each) sliced mandarin oranges, drained

In a large bowl, mix together the gelatin, cottage cheese, and whipped topping until well blended. Add the marshmallows and oranges.

Chill, covered, for 2 hours before serving.

Makes 4 servings

Per serving: *320 calories, 16 g protein, 39 g carbohydrate, 0 g fat, 5 mg cholesterol, 820 mg sodium, 2 g fiber*

Diet Exchanges: *0 milk, 0 vegetable, 1 fruit, 2 bread, 1 meat, 0 fat*

3 Carb Choices

SECRETS OF WEIGHT-LOSS WINNERS

- Doctor your veggies to make them delicious: Dribble maple syrup over carrots, and sprinkle chopped nuts on green beans. ***—Prevention* magazine**
- Make sure your plate is half veggies and/or fruit at both lunch and dinner. ***—Prevention* magazine**
- Start eating a big breakfast. It helps you eat fewer total calories throughout the day. ***—Prevention* magazine**
- Eat more soup. The noncreamy ones are filling but low-cal. ***—Prevention* magazine**

Bumble Berry Delight

—P. Dimmell, Lunenburg County, Nova Scotia, Canada

*"When I'm in the mood for something sweet, I like to make this.
It satisfies my cravings every time!"*

Prep time: 10 minutes
Cook time: 3 minutes

1 prepared boxed angel food cake mix
   (16 ounces)
½ cup strawberries, sliced
½ cup blueberries
1 apple, sliced
¼ cup honey

Prepare the cake mix according to the package directions.

In a medium saucepan over low to medium heat, combine the strawberries, blueberries, apple, and honey for 3 to 5 minutes, or until the fruit is soft. Remove from the heat to let the mixture cool completely.

Slice the cake, and top the slices with the fruit mixture.

Makes 8 servings

Per serving: *262 calories, 5 g protein, 62 g carbohydrate, 0 g fat, 0 mg cholesterol, 418 mg sodium, 1 g fiber*

Diet Exchanges: *0 milk, 0 vegetable, 0 fruit, 4 bread, 0 meat, 0 fat*

4 Carb Choices

237 Calories

Angelic Strawberry Trifle

—Kathy Christopherson, Oxford, Georgia

Prep time: 10 minutes
Chill time: 1 hour

1 **package (8 ounces) light cream cheese, softened**

1 **cup confectioners' sugar**

1 **teaspoon vanilla extract**

1 **container (8 ounces) frozen fat-free or light whipped topping, thawed**

4 **cups fresh strawberries, sliced**

1 **sugar-free angel food cake, cubed**

In a large bowl, use an electric mixer on medium speed to beat the cream cheese for 30 seconds, or until smooth. Slowly add the confectioners' sugar, a few spoonfuls at a time, and beat 1 to 2 minutes longer, or until the mixture is light and fluffy. Fold in the vanilla and whipped topping.

To assemble the dish, layer half of the cake cubes in the bottom of a large, clear bowl. Top with half of the cream cheese mixture and half of the strawberries. Repeat the layers. Cover and chill for 1 hour before serving.

Makes 8 servings

Per serving: *237 calories, 5 g protein, 46 g carbohydrate, 5 g fat, 13 mg cholesterol, 327 mg sodium, 3 g fiber*

Diet Exchanges: *0 milk, 0 vegetable, ½ fruit, 2½ bread, ½ meat, 1 fat*

3 Carb Choices

Fruit Salad

—Patsy Roy-Turple, Belledune, New Brunswick, Canada

107 Calories

"I love dessert, so instead of having a rich dessert I have a small bowl of fruit salad. It's the perfect way to enjoy fruit and have something sweet."

Prep time: 15 minutes
Cook time: 3 minutes

2 cups water

½ cup sugar

¼ cup apricot brandy

2 teaspoons lemon juice

1 apple, sliced

1 banana, sliced and peeled

2 kiwifruits, sliced

1 orange, peeled and sectioned

1 small bunch (about 4 cups) seedless grapes

½ melon, cubed (about 6 cups)

In a small saucepan, combine the water and the sugar and boil for about 3 minutes, or until the sugar has melted. Add the brandy. Let the mixture cool, then add the lemon juice.

In a large bowl, combine the apple, banana, kiwis, orange, grapes, and melon. Gently mix in the sugar water mixture.

Makes 16 servings

Per serving: *107 calories, 1 g protein, 25 g carbohydrate, 0 g fat, 0 mg cholesterol, 12 mg sodium, 2 g fiber*

Diet Exchanges: *0 milk, 0 vegetable, 2 fruit, 0 bread, 0 meat, 0 fat*

2 Carb Choices

Walnut Meringue Pie

—Renee Rewiski, Hawthorne, New Jersey

372 Calories

"This pie is low fat, and a small piece is satisfying. I make it for holidays and parties. If I have just a small piece, I'm happy and do not crave other, more fattening desserts."

Prep time: 15 minutes
Bake time: 30 minutes

20 reduced-fat Ritz crackers, finely ground
 1 cup walnuts, finely ground
 3 egg whites, at room temperature
 ½ cup granulated sugar
 ½ teaspoon baking powder
 1 teaspoon vanilla extract
 ½ container (8 ounces) fat-free whipped topping
 ¼ walnut halves

Preheat the oven to 350°F. Coat a 9" pie plate with cooking spray.

Place the crackers in a resealable plastic bag and crush them with a rolling pin.

Place the walnuts in the work bowl of a food processor and pulse for 1 minute, or until finely ground.

In a mixing bowl, use an electric mixer on medium speed to beat the egg whites for 2 minutes, or until soft peaks form. Gradually add the sugar and baking powder. Continue beating for about 3 minutes, or until stiff peaks form. Gently fold in the vanilla.

Fold in the crackers and walnuts. Pour the mixture into the pie plate, and bake for 30 minutes. Let the pie cool.

A well will form in the middle of the pie when it cools. Fill it with the whipped topping and garnish with the walnut halves.

Makes 8 servings

Per serving: *372 calories, 7 g protein, 50 g carbohydrate, 14 g fat, 0 mg cholesterol, 424 mg sodium, 2 g fiber*

Diet Exchanges: *0 milk, 0 vegetable, 0 fruit, 3½ bread, 1 meat, 2 fat*

3½ Carb Choices

Jenn's Easy No-Bake Prune Pie

—Jennifer Georgeff, Brantford, Ontario, Canada

147 Calories

"I have now lost a total of 80 pounds by making healthy, low-fat choices. This pie might sound strange, but it is very tasty, low in calories, and virtually fat-free without the crust. I tried it out with a group of people who loved it, and so will you!"

Prep time: 8 minutes
Chill time: 2 hours

1   **package (3 ounces) sugar-free lemon-flavored instant gelatin**

2   **cups prune juice**

½   **cup plain, fat-free yogurt**

1   **reduced-fat graham cracker pie crust, 9" in diameter**

¾   **cup frozen, fat-free whipped topping, thawed**

Lemon rind curls from 1 lemon (optional)

Sliced plums for garnish

Prepare the gelatin according to the package directions, but substitute the prune juice in place of water. Let the gelatin cool for 5 minutes. Whisk in the yogurt until the mixture is smooth. Pour the prune mixture into the pie crust. Chill in the refrigerator for 2 hours.

When the pie is chilled, cut it into slices and top each one with a tablespoon of whipped topping. Garnish with the lemon curls, if using, and top with the sliced plums.

Makes 12 servings

Per serving: *147 calories, 6 g protein, 26 g carbohydrate, 1 g fat, 0 mg cholesterol, 261 mg sodium, 1 g fiber*

Diet Exchanges: *0 milk, 0 vegetable, ½ fruit, 1½ bread, 0 meat, 0 fat*

2 Carb Choices

319 Calories

Pineapple Pie

—Suzie Lockhart, Angier, North Carolina

"This delightful pie has a nice, sweet taste without all the calories. I find it really refreshing on a hot day."

Prep time: 10 minutes
Chill time: 30 minutes

- 1 package (8 ounces) reduced-fat cream cheese, at room temperature
- 1 container (8 ounces) frozen, light whipped topping, thawed
- 2 cans (8 ounces each) crushed pineapple, well drained
- 1 reduced-fat graham cracker crust, 9" in diameter
- 2 cans (8 ounces each) pineapple chunks, well drained

In a large bowl, use an electric mixer on medium speed to beat the cream cheese for 2 to 3 minutes, or until it's smooth. Fold in the whipped topping, followed by the crushed pineapple. Pour the mixture into the crust. Top with the pineapple chunks. Chill for 30 minutes before serving.

Makes 8 servings

Per serving: *319 calories, 6 g protein, 50 g carbohydrate, 10 g fat, 16 mg cholesterol, 201 mg sodium, 3 g fiber*

Diet Exchanges: *0 milk, 0 vegetable, 1½ fruit, 2 bread, ½ meat, 1½ fat*

3½ Carb Choices

Light Strawberry Cheesecake

—Lily Erlic, Victoria, British Columbia, Canada

119 Calories

"This recipe gives me a delicious, great-tasting dessert that doesn't make me feel guilty."

Prep time: 7 minutes
Bake time: 30–35 minutes

  2 **full graham cracker sheets, crushed into crumbs**
  1 **package (8 ounces) light cream cheese**
  1 **package (8 ounces) light firm silken tofu**
  ½ **cup sugar substitute blend**
  2 **egg whites**
  1 **cup sliced strawberries**

Preheat the oven to 350°F. Place the graham cracker crumbs in a 9" pie plate. In a large bowl or food processor, blend together the cream cheese, tofu, sugar substitute blend, and egg whites for about 1 minute, or until smooth. Pour the mixture into the graham cracker crust. Bake for 30 to 35 minutes, or until set. Let the cheesecake cool. Garnish it with slices of fresh strawberries.

Makes 8 servings

Per serving: *119 calories, 6 g protein, 11 g carbohydrate, 5 g fat, 13 mg cholesterol, 213 mg sodium, 1 g fiber*

Diet Exchanges: *0 milk, 0 vegetable, ½ fruit, ½ bread, 1 meat, 1 fat*

1 Carb Choice

Almond Macaroons

—Billie Hudspeth, Tarpon Springs, Florida

"These cookies completely satisfied my sweet tooth."

Prep time: 10 minutes
Bake time: 17 minutes

1½ cups blanched almonds
 4 egg whites
1½ cups Splenda Sugar Blend for Baking
 1 cup unsweetened coconut
½ teaspoon vanilla extract

Preheat the oven to 300°F. Line a baking sheet with parchment paper.

Put the almonds in a food processor and pulse for 15 to 30 seconds, or until finely chopped. Beat the egg whites, using an electric mixer on medium speed for 2 minutes, or until stiff.

Gradually fold the Splenda and the almonds into the egg whites. Fold in the coconut and the vanilla.

Drop teaspoonfuls of the mixture onto the prepared baking sheet, placing them about 1" apart. Bake for 17 minutes.

Makes 52 cookies

Per cookie: *40 calories, 1 g protein, 2 g carbohydrate, 3 g fat, 0 mg cholesterol, 6 mg sodium, 1 g fiber*

Diet Exchanges: *0 milk, 0 vegetable, 0 fruit, 0 bread, 0 meat, 1 fat*

0 Carb Choice

Front left, *Peanut Butter Cookies (opposite page);*
Front right, *Banana Sunflower Cookies (page 236);*
Back, *20-Minute Quick Bread Cookies (page 239)*

Peanut Butter Cookies

—Rose Post, Overland Park, Kansas

"This recipe is low-carb, so it satisfies my sweet tooth without other, more sugary products."

Prep time: 12 minutes
Bake time: 12 minutes

1 cup low-carb peanut butter
1 cup Splenda Sugar Blend for Baking
1 egg

Preheat the oven to 350°F. Coat a baking sheet with cooking spray.

   In a large bowl, combine the peanut butter, Splenda, and egg. Roll the dough into tablespoon-size balls, and place them on the prepared baking sheet. Use a fork to press the balls flat, making a criss-cross pattern on the tops. Bake for 12 minutes.

Makes 14 cookies

Per cookie: *120 calories, 5 g protein, 5 g carbohydrate, 10 g fat, 15 mg cholesterol, 89 mg sodium, 1 g fiber*

Diet Exchanges: *0 milk, 0 vegetable, 0 fruit, 0 bread, 1 meat, 2 fat*

0 Carb Choice

Banana Sunflower Cookies

—Karin Buchanan, Westbridge, British Columbia, Canada

139 Calories

"These are cakey-type cookies that freeze beautifully and are delicious when reheated in a toaster or conventional oven. Otherwise, store them in a container with a loose-fitting lid, or the cookies will become soggy."

Prep time: 8 minutes
Chill time: 30 minutes
Bake time: 10 minutes

3 bananas, mashed
½ cup canola oil
½ cup granulated sugar
2 cups flour
1 cup sunflower seeds
1 tablespoon baking powder
1 teaspoon baking soda

Preheat the oven to 350°F. Coat a baking sheet with cooking spray.

In a large bowl, use an electric mixer on medium speed to cream together the bananas, oil, and sugar for 1 minute.

In a separate bowl, mix the flour with the sunflower seeds, baking powder, and baking soda. Add the flour mixture to the banana mixture. Mix thoroughly to combine. Chill in the refrigerator for 30 minutes.

Drop rounded tablespoons of the dough onto the baking sheet, placing them about 2" apart. Bake for 10 minutes, or until the edges are golden brown.

Makes 24 cookies

Per cookie: *139 calories, 3 g protein, 17 g carbohydrate, 7 g fat, 0 mg cholesterol, 104 mg sodium, 1 g fiber*

Diet Exchanges: *0 milk, 0 vegetable, ½ fruit, ½ bread, 0 meat, 1½ fat*

1 Carb Choice

SHOPPING SAVVY
Cookies

Think dieting means no dessert? Not any-more, thanks to Karen's Fabulous Tastes. She's baked up a new line of cookies that are sugar free (Karen uses Splenda), trans-fat free, wheat free, and pretty darn deli-cious. There are four cookie crisps: Heavenly Chocolate Chip, Caramel Dulce de Leche, Luscious Raspberry Almond, and Pecan Vanilla Praline, plus minimacaroons. We especially liked the pecan praline and dulce de leche crisps, and the Tropical Coconut macaroons. The cookies provide fiber, and, in general, 4 cookies add up to about 100 calories. Sold at supermarkets, gourmet shops, and natural food stores nationwide.

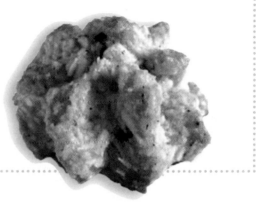

Meringue Cookies

7 Calories

—Linda Chaput, Rutherglen, Ontario, Canada

"Meringue cookies are best when they're still warm from the oven. They will keep in an air-tight container for 2 to 3 days."

Prep time: 5 minutes
Bake time: 1 hour 30 minutes

  3 egg whites, room temperature
⅛ teaspoon salt
½ teaspoon cream of tartar
⅓ cup granulated sugar

Preheat the oven to 200°F. Line a baking sheet with parchment paper.

In a mixing bowl, use an electric mixer on medium speed to beat the egg whites for 30 seconds, or until foamy. Add the salt and cream of tartar. Gradually add the sugar and beat for about 2 minutes on high speed, or until stiff.

Drop teaspoonfuls of the meringue onto the prepared baking sheet, placing them 1" apart. Bake for about 1 hour and 30 minutes.

Makes 46 cookies

Per cookie: *7 calories, 0 g protein, 2 g carbohydrate, 0 g fat, 0 mg cholesterol, 12 mg sodium, 0 g fiber*

Diet Exchanges: *0 milk, 0 vegetable, 0 fruit, 0 bread, 0 meat, 0 fat*

0 Carb Choice

SECRETS OF WEIGHT-LOSS WINNERS

• Use prebagged baby spinach everywhere: as "lettuce" in sandwiches, heated in soups, wilted in hot pasta, and added to salads.
—*Prevention* **magazine**

• Don't mistake thirst for hunger. Next time hunger pangs come on, start with a glass of water, wait 10 minutes, and see if that doesn't solve the problem.
—*Prevention* **magazine**

20-Minute Quick Bread Cookies

109 Calories

—Donna Knotts, Middletown, Delaware

"You can add raisins, dried fruit, nuts, sweetened coconut, or chocolate chips to this easy recipe, if you want. My favorite combination is banana bread mix with walnuts and coconut added."

Prep time: 10 minutes
Bake time: 10 minutes

- ½ cup trans-free margarine
- 1 package (13.9 ounces) quick bread mix (any flavor)
- 1 egg
- ¼ cup granulated sugar

Preheat the oven to 350°F. Line a baking sheet with parchment paper.

In a large microwaveable bowl, melt the margarine. Add the quick bread mix and egg. Mix well. Place the sugar in a small bowl.

Scoop out 1" balls of the dough and roll them quickly in the sugar. Place the dough balls 2" apart on the prepared baking sheet. Use a fork to flatten each ball, making a criss-cross pattern on the tops.

Bake for 10 minutes. Let the cookies cool for 2 to 3 minutes on the cookie sheet before transferring them to a rack to cool completely.

Makes 24 cookies

Per cookie: *109 calories, 1 g protein, 15 g carbohydrate, 5 g fat, 9 mg cholesterol, 138 mg sodium, 0 g fiber*

Diet Exchanges: *0 milk, 0 vegetable, 0 fruit, 1 bread, 0 meat, 1 fat*

1 Carb Choice

Brownie Nut Biscotti

—Barbara Price, Greenwich, New York

128 Calories

"Stored in air-tight containers, these crisp and nutty cookies will provide several weeks of enjoyment—if they last that long."

Prep time: 15 minutes
Bake time: 50 minutes
Cool time: 15 minutes

  4 tablespoons unsalted butter, softened
1½ cups Splenda Sugar Blend for Baking
1½ teaspoons vanilla extract
  4 large eggs
  1 tablespoon instant coffee crystals
  1 cup walnuts, chopped
  6 tablespoons unsweetened cocoa
     + additional for dusting
2½ cups whole wheat flour + additional for
     dusting
  ½ teaspoon salt
  2 teaspoons baking soda
     Cinnamon, for dusting
  ¼ cup white chocolate

Preheat the oven to 350°F. Coat 2 large baking sheets with cooking spray.

In a large bowl, use an electric mixer on medium speed to blend together the butter and the Splenda for 3 minutes. Add the vanilla and eggs, one at a time, mixing after each addition until well combined. Add the coffee, nuts, and cocoa, and beat until smooth.

In a separate bowl, sift together the flour, salt, and baking soda, then add it in batches to the butter mixture. (The dough should gather in a ball around the mixing blade and be firm but slightly sticky. Add a tablespoon of water if it seems too stiff; add an extra ¼ cup of flour if it seems too sticky.)

Turn the dough out onto a floured board, and gather it into a ball. Knead it briefly, until it holds together smoothly. Divide the ball into quarters.

Dust the board with equal portions of flour and cocoa and a sprinkle of cinnamon. Roll each quarter of the dough into a thick log, long enough to fit the length of your baking pan. Arrange 2 logs on each baking sheet. Bake for 25 minutes. Remove from the oven and reduce the oven temperature to 200°F. Let the logs cool on the trays for 15 minutes.

Transfer the logs to a cutting board and, using a long serrated knife (an electric bread knife is best), cut each log into ¼" slices. Place the slices back on the baking sheets just as they were before, leaving a slight amount of space between each slice. Bake for an additional 20 to 30 minutes. Let the biscotti cool completely.

Melt the chocolate in a microwaveable bowl. Let it cool slightly, and pour it into a baggie. Snip the corner of the baggie, and drizzle the chocolate onto the cooled cookies. Let it set before storing in an airtight container.

Makes 24 biscotti

Per biscotti: *128 calories, 4 g protein, 13 g carbohydrate, 7 g fat, 41 mg cholesterol, 169 mg sodium, 2 g fiber*

Diet Exchanges: *0 milk, 0 vegetable, 0 fruit, 1 bread, ½ meat, 1 fat*

1 Carb Choice

81 Calories

Protein Bites

—J. L. Heath, Laramie, Wyoming

"This is a healthy substitute for peanut butter cups or other nutritionally void snacks. They are tasty, and they're substantial enough to be satisfying. Plus they're packed with protein and vitamins!"

Prep time: 10 minutes
Chill time: 30 minutes

  1 cup peanut butter
  ½ cup dry powdered milk
  ½ cup honey
  1 cup shredded coconut
  ½ cup toasted sesame seeds

Line a baking sheet with waxed paper.

In a large bowl, combine the peanut butter, milk, honey, coconut, and sesame seeds. Roll the mixture into tablespoon-size balls, and place them on the prepared baking sheet. Refrigerate for 30 minutes.

Makes 40 bites

Per bite: *81 calories, 3 g protein, 6 g carbohydrate, 6 g fat, 0 mg cholesterol, 37 mg sodium, 1 g fiber*

Diet Exchanges: *0 milk, 0 vegetable, 0 fruit, ½ bread, 0 meat, 1 fat*

½ Carb Choice

Front left, *Low-Carb Chocolate Globs* (*page 244*)
and Front right, *Protein Bites* (*page 242*)

Low-Carb Chocolate Globs

—Niki Moyer, Altoona, Pennsylvania

"These tasty treats sure beat my craving for sweet items."

96 Calories

Prep time: 7 minutes
Cook time: 4 minutes
Chill time: 30 minutes

- 1 ounce unsweetened baking chocolate, chopped
- ½ cup low-sugar peanut butter
- 2 tablespoons reduced-fat cream cheese
- ¼ cup Splenda Sugar Blend for Baking
- ½ cup walnuts, chopped
- ¼ cup shredded unsweetened coconut

Line a baking sheet with waxed paper.

In a double boiler, melt together the chocolate, peanut butter, and cream cheese over very low heat. Remove from the heat and add the Splenda, nuts, and coconut. Drop tablespoon-size drops onto the prepared baking sheet. Roll in extra coconut, if desired. Refrigerate for 30 minutes to harden.

Makes 16 pieces

Per piece: *96 calories, 3 g protein, 3 g carbohydrate, 8 g fat, 1 mg cholesterol, 43 mg sodium, 3 g fiber*

Diet Exchanges: *0 milk, 0 vegetable, 0 fruit, 0 bread, ½ meat, 1½ fat*

0 Carb Choice

Strawberry Banana Popsicles

—Vanessa Bishop, Bolingbrook, Illinois

45 Calories

"When I want something cool, I reach for one of these refreshing treats. They're not filled with artificial sweeteners and preservatives, like store-bought popsicles."

Prep time: 5 minutes
Freeze time: 3 hours

  1 cup water
  1 cup skim milk
 15 strawberries, sliced
  2 ripe bananas, sliced
  1 tablespoon honey

In a blender, blend together the water, milk, strawberries, bananas, and honey for about 3 minutes, or until smooth. Pour the mixture into a popsicle mold, and freeze for at least 3 hours.

Makes 10 popsicles

Per serving: *45 calories, 1 g protein, 11 g carbohydrate, 0 g fat, .5 mg cholesterol, 11 mg sodium, 2 g fiber*

Diet Exchanges: *0 milk, 0 vegetable, 1 fruit, 0 bread, 0 meat, 0 fat*

1 Carb Choice

LeeAnn's Luscious Smoothie

—LeeAnn Dobro, Mansfield, Massachusetts

175 Calories

"I have tried to eliminate as much processed sugar as I can. This makes a sweet, filling meal, without sugar. It satisfies my desire for something sweet."

Prep time: 5 minutes

1 cup plain yogurt

1 banana, sliced

3 tablespoons wheat germ

5 frozen strawberries

¼ cup frozen blueberries (optional)

½ teaspoon vanilla extract

1 tablespoon fat-free milk

In a blender, combine the yogurt, banana, wheat germ, strawberries, blueberries (if using), vanilla extract, and milk for 40 seconds.

Makes 2 servings

Per serving: *175 calories, 9 g protein, 32 g carbohydrate, 2 g fat, 13 mg cholesterol, 84 mg sodium, 4 g fiber*

Diet Exchanges: *0 milk, 0 vegetable, 1½ fruit, ½ bread, 0 meat, ½ fat*

2 Carb Choices

Left, *LeeAnn's Luscious Smoothie (opposite page)*
and Right, *Slim-Down Smoothie (page 248)*

Slim-Down Smoothie

—Sharon Stirler, Tucson, Arizona

"This recipe makes a wonderfully thick and tasty smoothie, which easily substitutes for milkshakes and ice cream. Making this switch was easy, and I've been able to increase my daily intake of fruits and vegetables with one easy drink! The cauliflower won't change the flavor, but it will add body and nutrients to the smoothie, plus a serving of vegetables."

Prep time: 5 minutes

1¼ cups fat-free milk

¼ cup orange juice

¾ cup fat-free vanilla yogurt

⅓ cup fat-free whipped topping

½ cup frozen blackberries, strawberries, or raspberries

½ cup frozen cauliflower

In a blender, combine the milk, juice, yogurt, whipped topping, berries, and cauliflower for 1 minute, or until smooth.

Makes 2 servings

Per serving: *204 calories, 11 g protein, 38 g carbohydrate, 1 g fat, 5 mg cholesterol, 143 mg sodium, 3 g fiber*

Diet Exchanges: *½ milk, ½ vegetable, ½ fruit, 1½ bread, 0 meat, 0 fat*

2½ Carb Choices

Soy Good Smoothie

—Candace McMenamin, Lexington, South Carolina

305 Calories

"This helped me lose weight because it was a quick and easy way to make a breakfast that I could eat on the go. By not skipping breakfast, I didn't have to grab my usual 'junkie mid-morning' snack. I got calcium from the milk and two servings of fruits. The corn flakes added just enough carbs to give me a healthy boost in the mornings."

Prep time: 5 minutes

1 cup calcium-fortified vanilla soy milk
½ cup frozen blueberries
½ cup corn flakes cereal
1 frozen banana, sliced

In a blender, combine the milk, blueberries, cereal, and banana for 20 seconds. Scrape down the sides and blend for an additional 15 seconds.

Makes 1 serving

Per serving: *305 calories, 8 g protein, 74 g carbohydrate, 4 g fat, 0 mg cholesterol, 192 mg sodium, 6 g fiber*

Diet Exchanges: *2 milk, 0 vegetable, 2½ fruit, ½ bread, 0 meat, 0 fat*

5 Carb Choices

Watermelon Smoothie

—Laura Dixon, Hamilton, Ontario, Canada

"This smoothie is an excellent way to cool down."

Prep time: 10 minutes

  2 **cups chopped watermelon**
  ¼ **cup fat-free milk**
  2 **cups ice**

In a blender, combine the watermelon and milk for 15 seconds, or until smooth. Add the ice and blend for 20 seconds, or to your desired consistency. Add more ice if needed, and blend for 10 seconds.

Makes 2 servings

Per serving: *50 calories, 2 g protein, 15 g carbohydrate, 0 g fat, 1 mg cholesterol, 20 mg sodium, 1 g fiber*

Diet Exchanges: *0 milk, 0 vegetable, 1 fruit, 0 bread, 0 meat, 0 fat*

1 Carb Choice

World's Best Smoothie

—Dion Frischer, Ann Arbor, Michigan

288 Calories

"I have this smoothie almost every morning for breakfast, along with a piece of whole wheat matzo spread thinly with peanut butter and fruit-juice-sweetened jam. It is so satisfying that I have never felt deprived, and it satisfies me until lunchtime."

Prep time: 5 minutes

1 cup plain nonfat yogurt
1 banana
½ cup orange juice
6 frozen strawberries

In a blender, combine the yogurt, banana, juice, and strawberries for 20 seconds. Scrape down the sides and blend for an additional 15 seconds.

Makes 1 serving

Per serving: *288 calories, 12 g protein, 67 g carbohydrate, 0 g fat, 5 mg cholesterol, 138 mg sodium, 6 g fiber*

Diet Exchanges: *1½ milk, 0 vegetable, 3 fruit, 0 bread, 0 meat, 0 fat*

4½ Carb Choices

119 Calories

Sweet Banana Shake

—Sally Buckert, Katy, Texas

"This shake helps curb my hunger for sweets and acts as my evening dessert."

Prep time: 5 minutes

1 banana, sliced
½ cup fat-free milk
⅛ teaspoon nutmeg
1 packet artificial sweetener
½–1 cup ice cubes

In a blender, add the banana, milk, nutmeg, sweetener, and ½ cup of ice cubes. Blend for 15 seconds, adding additional ice cubes slowly until you achieve the desired consistency.

Makes 2 servings

Per serving: *119 calories, 7 g protein, 24 g carbohydrate, 0 g fat, 2 mg cholesterol, 96 mg sodium, 2 g fiber*

Diet Exchanges: *½ milk, 0 vegetable, 1 fruit, 0 bread, 0 meat, 0 fat*

1½ Carb Choices

Numi Tea

A small company, Numi Tea was founded by a brother and sister who traveled throughout Asia tasting and choosing teas for their exceptional line. Their teas, tea blends, and teasans (herbal blends) have fantastic names such as Rooibus, Monkey King Jasmine, Temple of Heaven, Morning Rise, Moonlight Spice, and Rainforest Green Lemon Myrtle. Most exotic are their artisan teas, which are tea leaves crafted and hand sewn into gorgeous rosettes. When steeped in water, they bloom open, releasing their flavor and aroma. Very soothing. Found at Whole Foods, Wild Oats, and some supermarkets. For a store locator, go to www.numitea.com.

Deluxe Milkshake (opposite page):
Front, *Chocolate;*
Middle, *Vanilla;*
Back, *Strawberry*

Deluxe Milkshake

—Syretta Patterson, El Paso, Texas

Prep time: 5 minutes

1 **cup low-fat ice cream, any flavor**
1 **cup fat-free milk**
4 **tablespoons fat-free whipped topping**
2 **maraschino cherries**

In a blender, combine the ice cream and the milk for 15 seconds. Top with whipped topping and a maraschino cherry.

Makes 2 servings

Per serving: *187 calories, 6 g protein, 33 g carbohydrate, 2 g fat, 7 mg cholesterol, 106 mg sodium, 1 g fiber*

Diet Exchanges: *½ milk, 0 vegetable, 0 fruit, 1½ bread, 0 meat, ½ fat*

2 Carb Choices

Dieter's Holiday Eggnog

—Janet Jackson, Hermiston, Oregon

126 Calories

"This has helped us to put a hold on holiday weight gain. The gelatin and sugar substitute will make your eggnog taste and feel as though it is sinfully rich, but it isn't."

Prep time: 10 minutes

¼ cup cold water
1 tablespoon unflavored gelatin
1 cup powdered fat-free milk
⅓ cup sugar substitute
2 large eggs
2 teaspoons vanilla extract
¼ teaspoon rum extract
1 teaspoon cinnamon
½ teaspoon ground nutmeg
¾ cup boiling hot water
2 cups ice water

In a blender, combine the cold water and gelatin. Let it sit for 1 to 2 minutes. Add the powdered milk, sugar substitute, eggs, vanilla extract, rum extract, cinnamon, and nutmeg. Blend on low for 30 seconds.

Add the boiling water and blend on low for 30 seconds, or until the mixture is thoroughly combined and the gelatin is dissolved.

Add the ice water and blend on high for 2 minutes.

Makes 4 servings

Per serving: *126 calories, 12 g protein, 12 g carbohydrate, 3 g fat, 106 mg cholesterol, 143 mg sodium, 0 g fiber*

Diet Exchanges: *1 milk, 0 vegetable, 0 fruit, 0 bread, 1 meat, 0 fat*

1 Carb Choice

Photo Credits

Front Cover
Mitch Mandel/Rodale Images

Back Cover
Mitch Mandel/Rodale Images

Interior
All recipe photos by Mitch Mandel/Rodale Images

© Melissa's: page 64
© Swanson: page 73
© OXO: page 105
© Fruit₂O: page 108
© Terra Medi: page 120

© Barilla Plus: page 170
© Eggology: page 203
© Bryer's: page 216
© Karen's Fabulous Tastes: page 237
© Numi Tea: page 253

Courtesy of Tessie Konya: page 46
Courtesy of Danny Schwartz: page 66
Courtesy of Barbara Orland: page 102
Courtesy of Paula Gebhart: page 115
Courtesy of Christina Alderman: page 125
Courtesy of Linda Lindsey: page 144
Courtesy of Margaret Roach: page 193
Courtesy of Trudy Rogers-Moore: page 205

Index

M